MW00934975

life skills for boys made easy (ages 9-12)

Easy Guide to Navigate Bullying, Peer Pressure, and Friendships While Boosting Communication, Confidence, and Mental Resilience

markus lucibello

© **Copyright Markus Lucibello 2024 - All rights reserved.**

The content within this book may not be reproduced, duplicated or transmitted without direct written permission from the author or the publisher.

Under no circumstances will any blame or legal responsibility be held against the publisher, or author, for any damages, reparation, or monetary loss due to the information contained within this book. Either directly or indirectly. You are responsible for your own choices, actions, and results.

Legal Notice:

This book is copyright protected. This book is only for personal use. You cannot amend, distribute, sell, use, quote or paraphrase any part, of the content within this book, without the consent of the author or publisher.

Disclaimer Notice:

Please note the information contained within this document is for educational and entertainment purposes only. All effort has been expended to present accurate, up-to-date, and reliable, complete information. No warranties of any kind are declared or implied. Readers acknowledge that the author is not engaging in the rendering of legal, financial, medical or professional advice. The content within this book has been derived from various sources. Please consult a licensed professional before attempting any techniques outlined in this book.

By reading this document, the reader agrees that under no circumstances is the author responsible for any losses, direct or indirect, which are incurred as a result of the use of the information contained within this document, including, but not limited to, — errors, omissions, or inaccuracies.

contents

introduction

Ever been the last one picked for a team, feeling like you're invisible? Sat alone at lunch, wondering why making friends seems like a puzzle you can't solve? Maybe you've felt nervous speaking up in class, even when you knew the answer. I've been there too, trust me.

And let's talk about those group chats and online games. Have you felt left out or worried about what to say? It's like everyone else got a handbook on being cool, and you're just trying to catch up. I get it. It's not just about fitting in; it's about figuring out this whole 'growing up' thing, which can be as confusing as a maze with no exit.

Especially when you get thrown curveballs by this beautiful thing called life. But guess what? You're not alone on this journey. Every boy your age is trying to solve the same puzzle – how to be confident, make real friends, and stand up to challenges, whether it's a bully in the corridor or that voice in your head doubting you. This book? It's like your personal guide, written by someone who's walked in your shoes and found the way out of the maze.

Okay, so you're thinking, 'All this sounds great, but how do I actually make it happen?' Well, the secret sauce is something called life skills. Yep, these aren't just any skills – they're like your Swiss Army knife for life. Think about it: landing your dream job someday? That's life skills in action. Raising a family or even just babysitting your little cousin? You guessed it, life skills. And nailing a class presentation or convincing your friends to try your epic game plan? All about those life skills.

Life skills are like unlocking your superhero gear – they boost your confidence, make you ace life's changes, and prep you for challenges like facing a bully. Here's how they turn you into a champ:

- **Be Your Own Hero:** These skills pump up your self-confidence, so you can tackle anything – from new schools to new challenges, like standing up to a bully.
- **Your Voice, Your Power:** Wanted to be heard loud and clear? Life skills give you that voice, making you a star in school now and a leader in society later.
- **Master of Your Universe:** You'll learn all about your rights and responsibilities. It's like training for future adventures, where you'll face challenges, grab opportunities, and solve problems like a pro.
- **Friend Magnet & Team Player:** Want to be the kid everyone looks up to? With these skills, you'll be making friends like a magnet and rocking teamwork like it's a video game.
- **Detective Mind:** Solve life's mysteries and puzzles with your sharp thinking and creative ideas.
- **Cold Master:** When things get tough, you'll stay as cool as your favorite ice cream, handling pressure like it's no big deal.
- **Convo Pro:** Chat, listen, and share ideas like you're hosting your own YouTube channel. Everyone will want to tune in!

I know you are thinking 'Okay, I get that these skills are good to have, but are they really necessary?' You bet they are! And I've got some amazing stories to prove it. These aren't just tales from a far-off land; they're real-life examples of people who used everyday skills to do extraordinary things. We're talking about the same skills that you will be learning in this very book!

Dwayne "The Rock" Johnson: His football dreams may have been dashed, but The Rock's resilience and adaptability shone through. He reinvented himself from a football player to a wrestler, and then to a successful actor, demonstrating the power of persistence and the ability to pivot and adapt to new challenges.

Jim Carrey: Growing up in poverty and working as a janitor, Carrey's unwavering belief in his dream and his unique comedic talent showcase his determination and self-belief. His ability to visualize success and stay committed, even in tough times, is a testament to his mental resilience and optimism.

Chris Pratt: Living in a van and struggling early in his career, Pratt showed incredible resilience and a positive attitude. His willingness to take on various jobs while pursuing acting illustrates his adaptability and work ethic, crucial skills that eventually led to his success in Hollywood.

Leonardo DiCaprio: DiCaprio's rise from a difficult childhood environment to a celebrated actor required immense perseverance and commitment. His dedication to refining his craft and his ability to overcome personal and financial challenges highlight his resilience and focus.

Robert Downey Jr.: Downey Jr.'s journey of overcoming addiction and rebuilding his career is a remarkable display of personal resilience, self-improvement, and determination. His willingness to seek help, learn from his mistakes, and commit to a better path demonstrates the importance of self-awareness and the courage to change.

These amazing stories of Dwayne Johnson, Jim Carrey, Chris Pratt, Leonardo DiCaprio, and Robert Downey Jr. are just the tip of the iceberg. There are many more inspiring tales out there, featuring celebrities like Oprah Winfrey, Keanu Reeves, and LeBron James, who have all transformed their lives through sheer resilience and determination.

But remember, it's not just about the famous faces. Think about the everyday folks – people like you and me – who have turned their lives around in incredible ways. We might not always hear about them, because their stories don't always make the headlines or fill the pages of a book like this one. But trust me when I say this: there are thousands of unsung heroes who, each single day, face hardships and flip the script to create better, brighter futures for themselves. Their journeys are a powerful reminder of the extraordinary potential that lies within each one of us, waiting to be unlocked with the right set of life skills.

Whoa, hold on a minute. After checking out all these awesome life skills and stories, you might be thinking, 'This sounds great, but where do I even start? How do I actually do all this?' Well, don't you worry!

Got that fire in your belly, the kind that sparks when you say, 'I've had enough, it's time to change things up'? That's the game-changer, the moment you decide you're ready to stand taller, speak louder, and show the world what you're made of. That feeling, right there, is why you're holding this book. You're not here for just another story; you're here because something inside you said, 'Let's do this!'

This book isn't just words on paper; it's your secret playbook, your behind-the-scenes coach cheering you on as you tackle the big stuff.

It's here because you decided you want to laugh louder, high-five your fears, and stride into each day like it's your personal victory parade. You're on a mission to be more you – more confident, more courageous, more connected.

You picked this book as your ally because you're ready to make moves, to shake off the dust and step into the spotlight of your own life. It's for those moments when you've felt overlooked in a crowd, or when your voice got lost in the noise. It's for every time you thought, 'I wish I could be that guy,' and now you're ready to be that guy.

So, let's turn those 'someday' dreams into 'starting now' realities. This book is your first step on an epic journey to discovering just how awesome you can be. You're not just reading; you're transforming. And it all starts with that spark inside you, saying, 'It's my time now.'

Before we start I want you to imagine this: You close the last page of the book and suddenly, it's like you've unlocked a new level in the game of life. You feel this surge of confidence that's almost electric. Walking into school, there's a new spring in your step, a grin that doesn't fade. Where you once hesitated, now you speak up, your words hitting the mark, earning nods and smiles. That project that seemed like a mountain? You conquer it like a champ.

The hallways that used to feel like a maze of anxiety? They're now your stage, and you're the star. Even those bullies, who seemed like invincible bosses in a video game, don't faze you anymore. You've got this shield of smart, calm confidence. You know how to turn their taunts into nothing more than background noise.

Life's not just a series of days anymore; it's an adventure, and you're the hero. This isn't just wishful thinking; it's your new reality, thanks to the skills and confidence you've gained. Your world has transformed, and it's brighter, bolder, and a whole lot more fun.

Ready to light up your world? Let's make it happen!

1 /
understanding bullying

Think about this: 1 in every 5 kids says they've been bullied at school. That's not just a random stat; it could be someone in your circle, maybe even you. But let's clear something up – what's bullying really about? Is it just a few mean words, or is there more beneath the surface? We're going to dig into what bullying truly is and arm you with the know-how to stand up against it. Ready to tackle this head-on? Let's jump in.

what is bullying?

Bullying is like someone trying to be the big boss in a mean way, often picking on others who find it hard to fight back. It's not just about pushing or hitting; it can be about threats, stealing stuff, or even just using words to make someone feel small. It can also be leaving someone out on purpose or spreading untrue stories.

Bullying can take many forms - from hitting and name-calling to excluding someone or spreading rumors. And with stuff like cyber-bullying, it's not just in the playground anymore; it can follow you home on your phone or computer.

It's a big deal, and it's really important to understand it so we can all help stop it. Remember, it's never cool, and everyone deserves to feel safe and respected.

types of bullying and their impact

Verbal Bullying:

Verbal bullying is like someone using words as weapons. It's when they call you names, tease in a mean way, or make jokes that hurt. It's about poking fun at your looks, your family, or beliefs. Sometimes, it's nasty comments about your body or even threats. It's someone trying to chip away at your confidence.

But here's the thing – those words, they're just air unless you give them power. Remember, you're in charge of who you are and how you feel, not them. So, when the words fly, stand tall, knowing you're way above any hurtful chatter.

Physical Bullying:

Physical bullying is when someone tries to boss around by using their strength or actions, like hitting, kicking, or even just making mean gestures. It's about making someone feel small or scared by hurting them or their stuff.

It's more than just a bruise or a broken pencil; it can really shake up how someone feels about themselves and their place in school or the world. It's serious stuff and leaves marks on the inside, not just the outside.

Cyberbullying:

Cyberbullying is like having a bully in your pocket. Instead of mean words in the schoolyard, it's mean texts, posts, or comments online. It can be someone spreading rumors on social media, sending nasty messages, or even making a group to leave someone out.

It's tough because it can follow you home from school, pop up on your phone, and make you feel like there's no escape. But just like with any bullying, it's important to remember it's not okay, and you're definitely not alone in dealing with it.

What are the Effects of Bullying?

When you're dealing with tough stuff like bullying, it can cast a long shadow, with effects that might be felt way beyond the school-yard. It's like carrying a heavy backpack of worries that can make even the simplest things feel really tough.

It can leave you feeling like you're always on edge, unsure of when the next mean comment or hurtful act will come. It's like walking on thin ice, never really knowing who's got your back. This constant worry can make it super hard to focus on school or anything else, really. It's like trying to play a game while someone keeps changing the rules. It might really shake things up both now and later. Right away, it might make you feel scared, lonely, or really sad.

You might not enjoy your favorite hobbies as much, have trouble sleeping, or find it hard to focus. Sometimes, it can lead to really serious stuff, like thinking about harming yourself. And if bullying sticks around for a long time, it can lead to feeling really down or stressed out even when you're older, make it harder to feel good about yourself, or even cause trouble with eating and sleeping. It's a big deal, and that's why it's so important to talk about it and find ways to make it stop.

And avoiding things that remind you of bullying might happen without even realizing that's what you're doing. It's all part of trying to handle the big feelings that come with these tough times.

That feeling of unease can lead to feeling alone or thinking pretty low of yourself. It's tough, but knowing what's going on is the first step to standing strong against it.

That's the silver lining – tackling bullying early can make a huge difference, lightening that load and paving the way for happier school days and a sunnier future.

Now that we've covered the effects of bullying, it's clear this isn't something to take lightly. I'm going to share a few examples that really highlight why we need to tackle bullying seriously, at all times. It's not just about the here and now; it's about shaping a happier, healthier future for everyone.

Verbal and Physical Bullying: Samantha's Story

Samantha's fifth grade year was a tough one, and it's a story that might sound familiar to some of you. There was a kid in her class who was really mean. We're talking about the kind of mean that goes beyond not sharing or cutting in line. This kid used scary words, the kind that can make your stomach twist into knots. Worse still, he would sometimes hit her. Can you imagine going to school every day, worrying about that?

Every morning, Samantha woke up with a feeling of dread. The thought of facing another day at school with that mean classmate made her wish she could just stay in bed. It's like when you're playing a video game and you keep getting beaten by the same level, except this was no game - it was her real life.

Samantha's mom was her superhero in this situation. She did what any concerned parent would do. She went to the school and even talked to the police to try and make things better. But you know how it is, sometimes things don't change overnight. It was frustrating for Samantha, feeling like she was stuck in this situation.

Now, here's where things start to turn around. Samantha got help from a special program called BACPAC. It's one of those programs that's all about helping kids who are having a hard time. They showed Samantha ways to feel stronger, both on the inside and the outside. It's kind of like leveling up in a game, where you gain new skills and start to feel more confident.

With BACPAC's help, Samantha learned how to deal with bullies and how to feel good about herself again. It wasn't an instant fix, but slowly, things started to get better. She began to feel less afraid and started to enjoy school more.

So, why am I telling you all this? Because Samantha's story is an important one. It shows that even when things seem really bad, there are people and programs out there that can help. It's about not giving up and finding the strength to overcome tough situations. And remember, if you ever find yourself in a situation like Samantha's, it's okay to ask for help. That's what brave people do.

Cyberbullying: Anonymous Stories

""*On December 17, 2010, my daughter was a victim of cyber bullying. There were four children involved in a chartroom within their e-mail accounts. One ring leader who seemed rather angry with my daughter started name calling, letting her know nobody liked her, and even went as far as wishing she would die in a hole. This obviously was a very hurtful conversation which led to my 11-year-old daughter to even consider death as an option. I thankfully monitor my child's accounts and was able to copy the conversation and bring this conversation to my child's school.*

They acted quickly and knew the severity of the situation. My hope is that there will be a positive outcome, and the four involved will have the opportunity to learn from this. Education and positive guidance are important tools to use as you do not want it to repeat, nor for you want it to fester in the minds of these young souls.""

- Father of 12 year-old girl from VA

""Our Pastor was texting our daughter early morning and late at night. Then started FB emails telling her to stay in contact however she could. He told her how horrible her family is and what liars we were. Told her we did things just to make her feel bad. We spent $35,000,00 to get a Permanent Injunction prohibiting contact for 10 years. Now he is suing us for his attorney fees.""

- Mother of 17 year-old girl from IL

""I stopped being friends with this girl who was just a bad influence on me, and she got a couple of her friends to hate me. On MSN they had a group chat room, and it was the two girls, and they were threatening to bully me at school, and I got scared about it. (The first girl) said if I came to school, she would beat me up during recess, so during that day I hid in the bathroom at lunch.""

- 12 year-old girl from AL

""I have an account on this site called Formspring, and what it was is I got cheated on by my ex, and someone was just like, 'You need to let him go,' and started cussing me out. People are harsh. People are very harsh. Then they were saying my articles suck.""

- 16 year-old girl from AL

""I broke up with this guy because I wanted to keep our relationship secret. So, after a week he all of a sudden started texting me and saying how me and my brother were brats and how I was a B****. He said some pretty nasty things. I asked him why he said it and he said it was because I broke his heart, and he was getting revenge from that. Me and my friends often get bullied it's one thing if it's at school but to bring it home was another. We have to stick up for each other. I thought school was supposed to be safe.""

- 16 year-old girl from USA

As you can see from multiple examples it's not just something you see in movies or hear about in stories. But the key thing is to act fast. If something online makes you feel bad, scared, or uncomfortable, talk to someone you trust – like your family, a teacher, or a coach.

They're like your personal team, ready to help you out. Remember, it's super brave to speak up and ask for help. And who knows, by taking that step, you might be helping someone else who's going through the same thing. Stay strong, and remember, you've got this!

strategies for dealing with bullies

Dealing with bullies is really tough, in fact, it might be one of the toughest things you've faced in your life so far. I know, because I've been there, just like you might be now. After reading those previous stories, you've probably realized how crucial it is to take the right steps. Here's what you can do:

Tell a Trusted Adult:

I know it might seem scary to talk about what's happening, especially when it's bullying. Even adults sometimes struggle to ask for professional help. But remember, there's no shame in speaking up.

When you talk to a responsible adult, things can start changing for the better. They know who to talk to and what to do. Your parents and teachers were kids too, and there's a good chance they've faced similar challenges. So, don't hesitate to share your experiences with them – they're there to help.

As a matter of fact, I just have the right story for this step. One from my own life. In 3rd grade, I had this experience with a boy who seemed like my best friend. Whenever I didn't do things his way, he'd stop talking to me. It went on until I talked to my parents. Things then began to change.

He stopped talking to me, and initially, I was really upset. I thought that was how friendships worked. Looking back, I see how ridiculous that was. Soon, I became happier and made a true friend, who's still my closest buddy after 15 years! That's why it's super important to talk to a trusted adult when things get tough.

Use the Buddy System:

Do you know what bullies fear the most? They're like video game villains who lose their power when they're up against a group. Bullies often target someone who's alone because it's their main power move. But if you stick with your buddies, it's like draining the bully's power and making their HP level drop quickly. Even if they try to pick on you, you've got your friends backing you up. It's a smart way to protect yourself and show the bully they can't push you around.

Control Your Emotions:

Bullies often feel more powerful when they see you getting emotional. It's totally normal to feel upset but showing it can sometimes give them the upper hand. One way to handle this is by practicing not to react visibly, like by crying or looking visibly angry. Cooling down strategies can be really helpful. For example, counting to 10, writing down what's bothering you, taking deep breaths, or just walking away. Keeping your face calm can also be a good tactic. Remember, staying composed can keep you off the bully's radar and take away their power.

Ignoring the Bully:

This step relates to the previous step. When dealing with a bully, it's important to assert yourself. Tell them clearly and firmly to stop, then walk away confidently. This shows you're not intimidated. Ignoring their remarks is key – act uninterested, like by texting someone or focusing on something else. Pretending you don't hear them and continuing with your activity also sends a message that their words don't affect you. By consistently showing that you're unfazed and not giving them the reaction, they're looking for, the bully will likely lose interest. Remember, your calm and composed response can be a powerful tool in diminishing their impact on you.

Talking with a Friend:

Talking with a friend can be as helpful as speaking with an adult. It's a great step to take. Even if they can't solve the problem, having a friend by your side can make you feel less alone. Sharing your troubles with a buddy can give you a sense of support and comfort. Remember, a problem shared is a problem halved, and just knowing someone is there for you can make a big difference.

what not to do

While dealing with a bully, it's normal to feel angry and want to fight back. But remember our previous steps about ignoring the bully? You might wonder, "How can I ignore them if they are physically hurting me?"

That's a valid question. In situations where you're physically threatened, your safety is the priority. It's important to get away from the situation and seek help from an adult immediately. Fighting back might seem like a quick solution, but it often makes things worse and could get you in trouble. Remember, there are better and safer ways to handle these situations.

Finding the right balance in dealing with bullies is key. You don't want to be too passive and let the bullying continue, but being too aggressive isn't the solution either. It's about standing up for yourself in a calm and confident way, without resorting to physical or verbal aggression.

By doing so, you show the bully that their behavior doesn't affect you, and you maintain your own dignity and safety. This middle ground is the "sweet spot" where you handle the situation effectively without escalating it.

Remember what we talked about ignoring the bully? It is crucial for you to keep a handle on your emotions so the bully can't get a rise out of you.

I get it, sometimes bullies just don't seem to stop even if you do all this. But don't worry, by the end of this chapter, you'll have some cool strategies up your sleeve for those extra tough situations. You'll be prepared and know just what to do.

Building Resilience Against Bullying

Self-esteem and self-respect pop up a lot in conversations, whether you're chatting with family, friends, or teachers. But what's the real scoop on self-esteem, and why does it matter so much? It's a topic that gets everyone thinking because it's all about how we see and feel about ourselves, and that's a big deal in our daily lives.

If you have high self-esteem, you feel good about who you are, believing you're important and deserving of love and respect. On the flip side, low self-esteem can make you feel like you're not that important or valued by others. It's all about how you see your worth in your own eyes.

Having strong self-esteem and self-respect is like having a shield in the face of bullying. When you feel good about who you are and respect yourself, it's harder for a bully's words or actions to hurt you.

You're more likely to stand up for yourself and less likely to believe the mean things they might say. It's about knowing your worth and not letting anyone shake that. Building this inner strength is a superpower against bullying.

The great news is self-esteem isn't set in stone; it can definitely grow! Whether you're a kid or an adult, there are loads of proven ways to give your self-esteem a boost. We're going to dive into some of these awesome strategies and see how they can help make a big, positive change. Let's get started!

Have you noticed how football players seem to carry themselves with loads of confidence? There's a secret behind that! Being involved in sports or any physical activity really boosts your self-esteem. It's about more than just getting fit; it's about feeling strong, capable, and sure of yourself.

You might lean towards solo sports like boxing, swimming, or gymnastics, or you might enjoy team vibes in football or baseball. It's all about what you like best. There's no wrong choice here – every sport has its own cool way of boosting your confidence. So, pick what feels right for you and dive in!

As your personal coach, I'd recommend considering martial arts training. It's not just about physical strength; it's a fantastic way to build discipline, respect, and self-confidence. Plus, it's a cool way to learn self-defense skills while staying active. Whether it's Boxing, Judo, or Brazilian jiu-jitsu martial arts can be a fun and empowering choice!

Diving into these activities is like discovering your own super formula. It's all about tapping into that inner superhero, kind of like Captain America, and uncovering your own unique strengths and powers!

Physical sports are awesome, but let's not overlook activities like drama club. It might surprise you, but drama's a powerhouse for building confidence. You learn to express yourself and even stand tall when you're not feeling it. And hey, hanging out more—whether it's with friends, at church, or other gatherings—can really brighten your day.

Having a supportive group around you is super important. It might feel a bit scary opening up, but it's totally normal. Remember, it's all about give-and-take—sharing your own stuff and also lending an ear to your friends. This balance makes sure everyone feels heard and supported, like a team sticking together.

It's not just fun; it helps you make more friends and get better at chatting and understanding people. Mixing it up with different activities is like adding secret ingredients to your superhero recipe!

Curious about things you can do solo to boost your self-esteem, confidence, and resilience? You're in luck! There are some awesome tactics you can try all by yourself, proven to make a big difference. Let's get started!

Letter to Yourself

Writing letters to yourself is a cool way to boost your self-esteem. Try writing to your future self about your goals, then look back at it later to see how you've grown. Or, write to your past self, giving a high-five for achievements and learning from oops moments. Don't forget a thank you note to present you, celebrating all the awesome things about you. It's like having a friendly chat with yourself on paper!

Transforming Negative Self-Talk Activity

Transforming negative thoughts to positive ones is powerful. When you find yourself thinking "I can't" or feeling not enough, write those thoughts down on the left side of the paper. Identify what triggers these feelings, like a tough test or a tricky day. Then, on the right side of the paper, flip the script! Change "I can't" to "I can" or "I'll give it my best shot". It's about shifting your mindset from doubts to a 'can-do' attitude, turning challenges into chances to grow and shine.

Gratitude Journal

Keeping a gratitude journal can really boost your self-esteem. Try writing down things that made you happy or people you're thankful for. Just a few lines each day or week about the good stuff can make a big difference.

such as, "Something that made me smile today was _____," or, "Two people I was grateful for today were _____ and _____ because _____." If writing isn't your thing, drawing what you're grateful for works too. It's all about spotting the sunshine in your day and feeling great about it!

Achievements Collage

Start by listing your achievements and proud moments, like awards or times you helped someone. Remember, overcoming challenges and learning from mistakes are also big wins! Maybe you improved in a subject at school, learned a new skill, or helped a friend in need. Each of these experiences is proof of your growth and resilience. Remember, every small victory counts and is worth celebrating!

Random Act of Kindness

You can boost your confidence by doing random acts of kindness every day for a week. Try small things like doing a chore for someone, holding a door open, writing a supportive note, sharing something, or comforting a friend who's feeling down. After this week, reflect on how these acts made you feel. Remember, building confidence is a journey, and these small steps can lead to big changes in how you feel about yourself.

interaction part

Now that we've learned so much, it's time to put our knowledge to the test with some imaginary scenarios that could very well happen in real life.

SCENARIO ONE

There is a new student, Layla, in your class. Layla is from another country, and she is still learning the English language. During the lunch break, you notice some students making fun of the way that

Layla speaks and sounds. You also hear them making fun of Layla's surname.

- What could you do to support Layla?
- What advice could you give Layla?
- How will you make sure that this type of issue doesn't happen again?

SCENARIO TWO

A student in your school, Nadine, uses a wheelchair. You overhear a student group saying that Nadine doesn't belong in the school as her wheelchair gets in the way and blocks the corridor. The group of students also use offensive names about Nadine relating to her disability.

- How would you support Nadine?
- What advice would you give to Nadine?
- How will you make sure that the issue doesn't happen again?

Now that you're equipped with lots of knowledge on handling bullying, it's time to put these new skills into practice. Remember, standing up to bullying is just the first step. Next up, we'll tackle another challenge you might encounter peer pressure. It's all about making the right choices, even when it's tough. But don't worry, we've got some great tips coming up in the next chapter to help you navigate through it. Stay tuned to learn how to confidently handle peer pressure!

2 /
navigating peer pressure

Have you ever felt like you had to do something because your friends said it was cool, even though you didn't really want to? Peer pressure can feel like you're trying to stand firm in a strong wave. In this chapter, we'll learn how to recognize peer pressure and staying true to yourself, even when everyone else is doing something different.

Peer pressure is when your friends or classmates try to get you to do something because they think it's cool, even if you're not sure about it or don't want to do it. For example, maybe your friends dare you to skip a class, try a video game that's meant for older kids, or make fun of someone else.

It's like feeling pushed to do these things because you want to fit in or because you're worried, they might not think you're cool if you don't. But it's important to think about what you feel is right and not just go along with something because everyone else is doing it.

It's completely normal to want to fit in with your friends and class-mates. Sometimes, this desire can lead you to give in to peer pressure because doing what others do seems like the easiest way to belong. But remember, the best approach is to stay true to yourself. It's fine to share the same interests as your friends as long as it feels right to you. Yet, always prioritize being yourself, even if it means standing out or making different choices than your peers.

Peer pressure can come in two main forms:

1-Direct Peer Pressure:

Direct negative peer pressure happens when your friends directly ask you to do something that might not be good for you. This type of pressure can be really tough to resist because you might worry about being teased or losing your friends if you don't go along with what they're asking. It's like being put on the spot, and the fear of not fitting in or being laughed at can make it hard to say no. But it's important to remember that true friends won't force you to do things that make you uncomfortable.

2-Indirect Peer Pressure:

Indirect negative peer pressure is less direct but can still strongly influence your decisions. It's about what you see and hear other kids doing. For example, if everyone is wearing a certain brand or playing a specific game, you might feel like you should too, just to fit in. Nobody might directly ask you to do anything, but there's this unspoken pressure to go along with the crowd. It's like feeling you need to keep up with others to be part of the group.

making independent decisions

It's super important to listen to your own voice when making decisions. Think of it like being the captain of your own ship. You get to decide which way to steer, even if others are going in a different direction. It's about knowing what you're comfortable with and what matches your own values. Sure, it's cool to consider what friends think, but in the end, your choices should reflect who you are. Trusting yourself is key to being confident and true to who you are. Remember, your voice matters a lot!

You might be wondering, "This all sounds great, but how do I actually start listening to my own voice?" Well, it's about taking a moment to check in with yourself.

Making decisions can be like going on an adventure in a video game. Here's how to do it:

- What's the Quest? First, figure out what decision you need to make. It's like choosing your mission.
- Options are Your Tools: Look at all the choices you have, like picking your gear before a big battle.
- Choose Your Weapon: Think about each option like evaluating your weapons - which one will help you win the level?
- Play the Game: Go with your choice and see how it plays out. It's like taking a leap in the game and learning from what happens next.

When you start making decisions on your own, it's a good idea to begin with small things. Like choosing what outfit to wear for the day, picking out a healthy snack, or cleaning up your space.

These might seem like little choices, but they're actually big steps in building your confidence. Each time you make a small decision, it's like leveling up in being independent. And the more you practice, the better you'll get at making bigger decisions later on.

A consequence is what happens because of something you do. It's like the end result of your actions, whether good or bad.

Thinking about what happens after you do something is super important. Like, if you keep your room tidy, you won't have to search for your toys. Or if you wait your turn in a game, it's way more fun for everyone. And, putting on shoes keeps your feet clean. It's all about making smart choices to avoid tricky situations!

positive influences and choosing the right friends

We've talked about dealing with peer pressure, but let's not forget about the people who positively influence us. It's cool to know who's got your back, guiding you to make awesome choices.

Spotting these helpers is key – they're the ones who cheer you on, respect your choices, and are there to give a helpful nudge in the right direction! Let's figure out how to spot those awesome people who positively influence us.

When you look around yourself these persons might be positive influences that can come from various sources such as family, friends, teachers, or even characters in books or movies.

Role models in your life are super important. They're the ones who show you how to act cool and kind, respect others, and make smart choices. They're there cheering you on, pushing you to give your best, and making sure you feel awesome about yourself.

Plus, they're all about good habits, like munching on healthy snacks, staying active, and getting plenty of sleep. It's like having a guide to being your best self! Just like this book but alive!

Good friends are like treasure. They're there for you, remember the big stuff, and always lend a hand or an ear when you're down. They talk kindly, respect your feelings, and you can totally trust them. You'll probably like the same stuff, which is super cool.

Having the right friends around you is like being part of a super-hero squad. They teach you empathy, teamwork, and problem-solving. But not all friendships are smooth. Sometimes, challenges like bullying can make things tough.

That's why schools have special programs to help everyone learn how to support and understand each other. And if friendship issues get tricky, there's extra help to coach you on making and keeping positive relationships. Friends can be a big part of your journey, helping you become the best version of yourself!

Plus, they always think the best for you and stand strong by your side against bad things. That's what real friendship is all about!

You've explored the power of surrounding yourself with the right people. Now, get ready for some real-life stories, including ones about celebrities, which highlight just how much the company you keep can shape your journey. These tales are not only inspiring but also show the real impact of positive influences. Stay tuned for some eye-opening experiences!

Sophie

Sophie felt neglected at home, often alone while her parents struggled with their own issues. School provided some escape, but the loneliness and challenges persisted. Despite trying to speak up, she felt unheard and misunderstood, leading to moments of deep despair. This difficult period underscored her desire for change and understanding.

Sophie found hope with the NSPCC, who recognized her distress and helped her open about her feelings. She learned it wasn't her fault her mom used drugs and focused on making positive choices. With new coping strategies and a supportive network, Sophie's now building a hopeful future, planning for university, and living independently, showing the transformative power of guidance, and understanding.

Eminem: This rapper had a tough time with addiction. But guess what? He got help from his friends and rehab and turned things around. It's like having a team in a game to help you win the battle.

J.K. Rowling: Before she became famous for Harry Potter, she had a hard time with money and felt really sad. But she didn't give up because she had people who supported her and look at her now!

Robert Downey Jr.: Iron Man himself had problems with addiction and got into trouble. But he made an awesome comeback with help from friends and experts. It shows that you can always turn things around.

Demi Lovato: She's a singer and actress who faced challenges with her mental health. Thanks to her friends, family, and professionals, she made a great recovery. It's like having a super team to help you when you're down.

Just like Eminem, J.K. Rowling, Robert Downey Jr., and Demi Lovato, you'll face challenges too, because that's part of being human. But what really matters is that you don't give up. Surround yourself with good people, like friends and family who care about you. They'll help you get through tough times and come out stronger. Remember, every problem you face is a chance to show how tough and brave you can be!

Just like the real-life stories of famous people, there are awesome podcasts out there that can teach you more. My favorite is "The Big Life Kids Podcast." It shares inspiring stories about real-life role models who have overcome challenges. In each episode, characters Leo and Zara explore the world, learn about growth mindset strategies, and hear about others' experiences. It's a cool way to learn and get inspired!

But wait a minute, what exactly is a growth mindset? Here's a little explanation:

Growth Mindset vs Fixed Mindset

Imagine you're playing your favorite video game. If you have a fixed mindset, you might think, "I'm either good at this game, or I'm not." And if you keep losing, you might just give up.

But if you have a growth mindset, you think, "Hey, I can get better at this game with practice." You don't give up, even when it gets tough. You learn from your mistakes, try different strategies, and keep going. That's what a growth mindset is all about!

Now, think about school. If you find math hard, a fixed mindset might make you think, "I'm just bad at math." But with a growth mindset, you'd think, "I just need to practice more, and I can get better at math."

People with a growth mindset are like explorers. They love to learn, aren't afraid of challenges, and know that making mistakes is just part of getting smarter. They believe that their brain can grow stronger and smarter with effort, just like a muscle.

On the other hand, people with a fixed mindset are like they're stuck in a room with no doors. They think their skills and intelligence are just what they're born with and can't change much. They might avoid trying new things because they're afraid to fail.

So, why is having a growth mindset so awesome? Because it helps you to keep getting better at things, whether it's sports, video games, learning an instrument, or doing well in school. It's about not being afraid to try new things and not getting bummed out by a setback.

Imagine if your favorite superhero thought, "I can't save the world; it's too hard." They wouldn't be very super, right? But superheroes keep trying, no matter what. That's a growth mindset in action!

So next time you're learning something new or facing a tough challenge, remember to think like a superhero with a growth mindset. Tell yourself, "I might not be able to do this yet, but with practice and hard work, I'll get there." This way, you can conquer any challenge, just like a hero in your favorite game or comic book!

As you can see, a growth mindset is something everyone should aspire to have! It's all about believing that you can always grow and get better at things with effort and learning.

interaction - reflection journal

As you know from Chapter 1, it's important to apply what we learn. it's time to put that knowledge into action right away – that's how it really sticks! Below, you'll find around 33 questions about peer pressure.

These are designed to get you thinking in new and different ways about this topic. So, get ready to engage your brain like never before about peer pressure!

Before you start, don't forget that you don't have to go through all of this at once. It is also important to fully understand what you just read as well.

1. Imagine a friend wants you to skip school. What would you do?
2. What if a group of friends is laughing at someone else? How would you respond?
3. Have you ever felt pressured to change the way you look to fit in?

4. What would you say if someone pressured you to keep a secret from your parents?
5. How do you decide when to go along with what friends are doing or to do your own thing?
6. Have you ever done something you later regretted because of peer pressure?
7. If a friend dared you to do something unsafe, how would you handle it?
8. How would you support a friend who's struggling to stand up to peer pressure?
9. Do you think it's easy or hard to be yourself around your friends? Why?
10. What do you think is the best way to handle a situation where friends are pressuring you to break rules?
11. How do you feel when someone tries to pressure you into doing something you don't want to do?
12. Have you ever felt proud of yourself for not giving in to peer pressure? What happened?
13. What advice would you give to someone who's worried about peer pressure?
14. How can you tell the difference between good and bad peer pressure?
15. Can you think of a time when following your friends led to something positive?
16. What would you do if your friends asked you to do something you're not comfortable with?
17. How do you feel when you make a decision that's different from what your friends are doing?
18. Can you think of a time when you said no to peer pressure? How did it make you feel?
19. What are some ways you can say "no" to friends without feeling awkward?
20. How would you help a friend who's facing peer pressure?

21. What's more important: being popular or being true to yourself?
22. Can you think of a time when following the crowd led to trouble?
23. What would you do if your friends teased you for not joining in on something you knew was wrong?
24. How can you tell if someone is being a true friend or just pressuring you?
25. Can you give an example of positive peer pressure?
26. How would you handle a situation where your friends want to play a game you think is too aggressive?
27. What if your friends make fun of someone else's hobbies or interests? How would you react?
28. Have you ever felt pressured to change your opinion to match your friends'?
29. If you saw a friend giving in to peer pressure, how would you help them?
30. How do you think peer pressure affects your choices about what you watch or listen to?
31. What are ways to politely refuse something you don't want to do, even if all your friends are doing it?
32. Have you ever had to choose between doing what's right and being accepted by your friends?
33. If your friends were all buying something expensive, would you feel pressured to buy it too? How would you handle that?

Alright, guys! In Chapter 2, we went on a cool journey about handling peer pressure. We checked out how sometimes friends can push us to do stuff we're not cool with and learned the difference between direct and indirect pressure. It's like choosing your path in a video game – sometimes tricky, but you've got the controls. We talked about listening to your own thoughts and making choices that feel right for you.

Remember, small decisions like what to wear or eat matter too. And we discovered how awesome it is to have friends who really get you and help you make great choices. Just like some famous people we talked about, having the right crew can make all the difference. So, keep your heads up and steer your own ship through this adventure of growing up!

Now that you've learned all these cool things about handling peer pressure, it's your turn to give it a try! Remember, it's all about staying true to who you are and making choices that feel right to you. Don't forget to lean on your friends and family when things get tough – they're your team! Try out these ideas in your daily life and see how strong and confident you can be. You've got this!

Great job on learning how to tackle peer pressure! Next up, we're going to explore something super important in your life – friendships. Friendships can be awesome, but sometimes they can be a bit tricky too. In the next chapter, we're going to dive into how to make and keep great friends. You'll learn tips on being a good friend and how to handle friendship challenges. Get ready to discover more about the cool world of friendships!

3 /
fostering strong friendships

Think about your best buddy. What's the secret ingredient in your friendship? Sure, fun times count, but there's more, right? This chapter isn't just about finding friends; it's about being the friend everyone values. Ready to dive into the world of awesome friendships and learn how to make and keep them strong? Let's roll!

Having supportive friends is super important. They're like your personal cheer squad, always there to lift you up when you're down and celebrate your wins. When you've got friends around, even big challenges seem smaller. It's all about having someone by your side, making the tough stuff easier to tackle!

Having friends is not just good for laughs; it's great for your health too! People with strong friendships tend to live longer and stay healthier. Plus, having pals around can make your heart happier and keep stress away. It's like friendship is a secret health boost!

They can influence you to try new things, stick to healthy habits, and even help you dodge trouble. It's all about having those positive vibes around you, steering you toward the best paths!

Sometimes, just one good friend makes all the difference. They can shield you from the rough stuff and boost your self-esteem. More friends don't always mean more confidence; it's the quality of friendship that really counts.

Good pals can help your grades and overall happiness. Plus, when your friends are into good stuff, you're likely to follow suit and make great choices too. It's all about that good influence!

Friends are important, but it's true that both you and your friends might have tough days feeling sad. On those days you have to remember that they are there for you!

Opening up to friends might feel tricky, but remember, true friends are there for you, rain or shine. Sharing what's on your mind can make a big difference.

For a heart-to-heart, pick a comfy spot or chat over a message or call if that feels better. And just like you might need them, be ready to be their support too. It's all about being there for each other!

Just being there for your friend can mean a lot. Taking the time to chat, text, or hang out shows you care.

It's not about solving all their problems but listening and showing compassion. Friends aren't looking for you to be a therapist; they just value your support.

Sometimes, you might need to change your hangouts to suit their comfort, but keeping things normal is key.

Taking care of a friend can sometimes feel overwhelming. It's okay to take a break. This helps maintain your well-being and keeps the friendship healthy. Remember, it's about balance and mutual care.

how to be a good friend

Being a great friend is like being on a mission in your favorite video game; you're there to help each other through the tough levels. Just like keeping your gadgets in top shape, friendships need care too— like really listening, showing empathy, and being someone, your friends can rely on. Ready to level up your friendship game? Let's dive into what it takes to be that AMAZING friend!

Tips for how to be a good friend:

These are the tips we learned from mental health experts.

1. Prioritize making time for each other.

Being a good friend means valuing your time together. It's not just about hanging out; it's about creating shared memories and experiences that bring you closer. Look for fun, new ways to enjoy your time together, making every moment count. It's about making sure your friend knows they're a top priority in your life!

2. Open up and allow each other to be vulnerable.

Being a good friend means being real with each other. It's about letting your guard down, sharing your feelings, and knowing you'll be heard and supported. True friends stand by each other, ready for fun or comfort, and respect each other's limits. It's about trust and feeling safe together.

"Being able to have fun and share special memories are the result of having a trusting relationship that feels safe," Cristerna adds. "For example, all of my friends and I have an understanding that we support one another in every way (yes, even ridiculous ways!), unless the level of

ridiculousness is too much or would create a situation where we feel uncomfortable."

3. Pay attention to the little things.

Being a great friend means noticing even the small stuff. It's about really listening and understanding, so when a friend says 'OK' but you sense they're not, you're there to offer support. It's those little details that show how much you care.

"A good friend is able to read between the lines of what's being said because they pay attention, and they know your heart," Thompson says. "For example, if I ask, 'How are you doing?' to a close friend and the response is 'OK,' I know immediately that she is not OK. A good friend pays attention to the details because you care to take the time to understand the heart of your friend."

4. Be willing to challenge each other.

A true friend will encourage you to be your best, guiding you gently if you stray off track, all with love and respect. It's about helping each other grow and being there every step of the way.

"In a personal story, I was angry with someone, and one of my good friends stopped me midway through my rant and said, 'Jinnie, you know you're wrong. I am always with you, but on this one, I can't ride with you. Stop and think about the role you played in this.' That moment stays with me to this day because she loved me enough to tell me to knock it off, and it came from a place of love. I was able to receive it because of that," Cristerna explains. "That's what friends do."

5. Be open-minded.

Being a good friend means keeping an open mind, letting your buddy be themselves, and respecting their choices. It's about understanding and supporting them without pushing your own views. That's how friendships grow stronger!

6. Be their backup

As a good friend, you're like a guardian. In tough times, you're there to protect your friend's reputation, ensure their safety, or help them navigate tricky situations. It's about having their back and showing true friendship through actions, not just words.

If we were to make a small list to summarize :

- Checking in: If it's been a while, reach out. It shows you care.
- Expressing gratitude: Let them know you treasure the friendship.
- Listening well: Be the ear they need, offering your full attention.
- Celebrating and supporting: Cheer for their wins and offer a shoulder during tough times.
- Being there: In critical moments, your presence can mean the world.
- Forgiving: Everyone slips up. Don't hold grudges.
- Showing empathy: Understand their feelings and show compassion.
- Communicating openly: Honesty strengthens trust.
- Spreading joy: A good laugh can lighten any mood.
- Stepping in when needed: If their health is at stake, don't hesitate to help.
- Honest: They value truth and openness, even when it's tough.
- Nonjudgmental: They understand you, creating a space where you're free to be yourself.

- Accepting: They respect your life choices, recognizing everyone's path is unique.
- Trustworthy: They're your safe place, where secrets and dreams are securely kept.
- Low maintenance: They get that life is busy and value the quality of friendship over constant contact.

Alright, we've covered how to be a good friend in general. But you're thinking, 'What about the specific things I can say or do?' Don't worry, I've got you covered! Your personal friendship coach is here with some handy tips and tricks to level up your friendship game.

What to Say

1. "I'm here for you."

Telling a friend "I'm here for you" means a lot. It's a simple way to show support and let them know they're not alone. For an extra touch, say "I'm here for you when you're ready," to show you're there on their terms, building trust and offering a shoulder to lean on whenever they need it.

2. Small acts of kindness.

Acting is sometimes better than just talking, especially when it comes to helping friends feel better. A simple act, like bringing your friend their favorite snack, can really show you care, even if they're not ready to chat about their feelings. This small gesture can make a big difference to someone who's having a tough time.

3. "How can I help take your mind off things?"

Sometimes, friends just need a break from thinking about tough stuff all the time. You can be a super friend by helping them take their mind off things without needing to talk about it.

Doing something fun together, like watching a movie, going to a sports game, hanging out at their favorite park, working out together, or cooking a meal can really lighten their day. It's all about giving them a little escape and showing you're there for them in different ways.

4. "You want a hug?"

Just like bringing someone their favorite snack, a hug can be a powerful way to show you care without needing a lot of words. But remember, hugs are best for friends or family who are okay with it, and always make sure they're cool with a hug first. When it's the right time and place, and they're up for it, a hug can really help someone feel supported and less alone.

5. "I don't know but I'll do my best to help you"

Saying "I don't know, but I'll do my best to help you " is a great way to support your friend without giving advice they didn't ask for. It shows you're there for them, ready to tackle challenges together, even if it takes time. Being a good listener, or a sounding board, is super helpful, as long as your friend is okay with it.

6. "Do you want to talk about it?"

Always check with your friends first if they feel like talking about what's bugging them. They might not be ready, or it might not be the right time. Asking them shows you respect their space and won't push them to share if they're not up for it. And if they feel like they have to talk but don't really want to, it's cool to let them know, "Hey, it's totally okay if you don't want to talk about it."

7. "I thought of you when…"

Ever seen something and immediately thought of your friend, like a hilarious meme, a catchy TikTok, or their favorite song? Next time that happens, why not let them know? Sharing something because it reminded you of them is a sweet way to show they're on your mind. It's a simple gesture that says, "Hey, I'm here for you," and more importantly, "You're important to me."

8. "That sucks."

Sometimes friends just need to talk about what's bugging them, not looking for solutions but just wanting someone to listen. When you're there to hear them out, you're not just being a good listener; you're also showing you understand and care. This kind of support is a big deal—it shows empathy and encourages them just by acknowledging what they're going through.

what about bad friends and how to spot them?

Now you've got the scoop on being a great friend and what to expect in return. But what about those not-so-good friends? They're not always easy to spot right away. Up next, we've got some top tips to help you identify them early on, so you can steer clear and stick with the true pals!

Be cautious if:

- You often feel tired after talking to them.
- They only talk about themselves.

- They don't listen or give you space to speak.
- Your time or personal limits are ignored.
- They don't respect how you feel.
- They make you feel small or unimportant.
- The friendship feels too dependent on them feeling good and getting their way.

resolving conflicts in friendships

Ever suddenly found yourself in a disagreement with your buddy, feeling like they just don't get you at all? It's something that happens in friendships more often than you'd think.

But hey, it's not the end of the world! We're about to dive into some cool ways to fix things up and keep your friendship as awesome as ever. Get ready to learn how to understand each other better and move past those arguments, making your friendship even stronger!

Have you ever thought about why you and your friends might get into arguments? It's key to understand what kicks off those fights in the first place.

Knowing why can help us dodge those clashes and keep our friendships awesome. So, let's get into figuring out those reasons, helping you and your friends stay on the same page and keep the good times rolling.

Arguing might happen for a bunch of reasons. Here are some of them that you might recognize:

- Feeling left out
- Getting the wrong end of the stick
- When what's important to you changes
- Liking different stuff
- Just not clicking personality-wise
- When trust gets broken

- Someone being mean or bullying
- Drifting apart
- Getting jealous
- Not seeing eye to eye on things
- Feeling betrayed
- When someone's being manipulative
- Having different beliefs or values
- Pressure from other friends
- Trying to outdo each other
- Changes in who hangs out with whom

As you can see, there are lots of reasons why, but it doesn't stop here as well. It's also incredibly important HOW we argue. While we are arguing its crucial to :

Stay Cool: Take a moment to breathe and chill before you respond. Understand what's really going on first.

Be Nice: No name-calling or getting rough. Keep it respectful.

Feel Your Feelings: It's okay to have feelings, just recognize them without acting on impulse.

Really Listen: Sometimes your friend just wants to know you're listening. Make them feel heard.

Don't Snap Back: Skip the urge to get back at them or say something mean.

Time Out: If things are getting too heated, it's okay to walk away and cool off.

Keep It to Yourself: Don't blast your argument all over social media or tell the whole world.

Solve It Solo: Try to work things out without dragging others into it.

After you've had a disagreement with a friend, it's cool to take a step back and chill for a bit. Once you're feeling calmer, it's a good idea to think things over. Ask yourself a few questions to get a clearer picture:

- Did I overreact?
- Is this argument worth risking our friendship?
- What exactly made me feel upset or angry?
- Who else can I chat with about this?
- What do I wish my friend would do or not do?
- What do I need to move past this issue?
- What's bugging me the most about our argument?
- Did I do something to make the disagreement worse?
- How do I want things to be between us now?
- Could something be going on with my friend that I don't know about?

These questions can help you figure out your feelings and what to do next and when it's time to solve these arguments don't forget to :

1- Open and Honest Communication: Talking things out is super important when you're having trouble with a friend. Make sure to share what you're feeling in a cool, calm way. Try not to point fingers or make your friend feel bad. Instead, talk about your feelings with "I" statements like "I feel left out when I'm not included in plans" or "I get upset when it seems like I am not listened to."

This helps your friend understand where you're coming from without feeling blamed, making it easier for both of you to talk honestly.

2- Active Listening: Really listening to your friend is super important. When they're sharing their thoughts, give them all your attention. Don't interrupt or just wait for your turn to talk.

Try to really get where they're coming from and show you understand by repeating back a bit of what they've said. This shows you respect and care about their feelings, and it can really help cool things down if you're both upset.

3- Find Common Ground: When you're butting heads with a friend, it's easy to focus on what you disagree on. Try finding things you both agree on instead. This can help smooth things out and lead to a solution that works for everyone. Like if you're deciding where to eat, think about what foods you both like and pick a place that has them. It's about working together to find the middle ground.

4- Practice Empathy: Understanding your friend's feelings is key. Try seeing things from their perspective. It'll help you get why they might feel a certain way. Showing empathy means you're really listening and care about their feelings, paving the way to sort things out together.

5- Take Responsibility: In any mix-up, it's cool to admit if you've messed up. It's not about blaming yourself for everything but understanding how you've played a part and saying sorry if needed. It shows you're ready to fix things and move forward together.

6- Seek a Neutral Mediator: Sometimes, it's tough to hash things out by yourself. That's where bringing in a neutral mediator can be a game-changer. Think of them as the cool, unbiased friend or a pro who knows just how to untangle messy situations.

They're there to keep the peace and make sure everyone's voice gets heard. Whether it's a buddy you both trust, a counselor, or someone who does this for a living, they're all about helping you both find that sweet spot where everyone's happy.

7- Take a Break to Cool Off: You know those moments when everything gets too heated, and words just fly out before you even think? We've all been there. It's totally okay to hit the pause button if you feel things with your buddy are getting too intense. Taking a breather gives both of you some space to chill and clear your heads.

While you're on this little timeout, do something that shakes off the stress. Maybe take a walk, lose yourself in some meditation, or just chat with someone who gets you. Once the storm inside calms down, it's way easier to come back and chat it out with your friend, all cool-headed and ready to sort things out together. Sometimes a little space is all you need to see things in a new light!

8- Brainstorm Solutions Together: Alright, once you've both laid everything out on the table and really heard each other, it's time to put on those thinking caps together. Think of it like a team effort to fix a puzzle where both of you matter. Toss around ideas, be open to what the other person's pitching, and let those creative juices flow.

This isn't about sticking to your guns and refusing to budge. It's about finding that sweet spot where both of you can nod and say, "Yeah, that works." Keep in mind, it's not about who wins the argument. It's all about keeping that friendship golden and making sure you both walk away feeling good about how you've handled things. So, dive into that brainstorm and start building that bridge back to each other!

9- Follow Up and Follow Through: Remember, smoothing things over isn't just a one-and-done chat. It's more like keeping a tune-up on a friendship. After you've both agreed on how to move forward, don't just leave it at that. Circle back after a bit and see how things are holding up. Need to tweak something? No problem, that's what check-ins are for. Stick to the promises you made – it's like saying, "Hey, I value our friendship enough to make this work." It's about showing up, not just in the tough talks but in the days and weeks that follow.

This way, you're not just patching things up for now, but you're also laying down the tracks for a solid, lasting friendship. So, keep that communication line open and keep caring. That's how you turn a rough patch into a stronger bond.

crafting the ultimate friendship potion: communication, compromise, and forgiveness

So, you already know that talking things out is like the secret code for an awesome friendship. But guess what? We've got two more cool tricks up our sleeve to make your buddy bond super strong! Next up is Compromise – that's when you and your pal figure out how to give a little, take a little, and find that sweet spot where everyone's happy.

And the final awesome ingredient? Forgiveness. It's like having a superpower to erase any grudges and keep your friendship as fun as a game on the highest level. Mix Talking, Teaming Up, and Letting Go together, and boom – you've got the ultimate friendship potion that'll make your bond unbeatable! Ready to whip up this wicked brew and become friendship wizards? Let's get to it!

Learning the Superpower of Forgiveness

Did you know learning about forgiveness is like getting yourself a superhero cape? It's true! When you learn to forgive, you're not saying it's okay when someone does something not-so-cool. What you're really doing is deciding not to let those icky feelings hang around and ruin your day. Forgiveness is like a superpower that helps you feel more understanding, caring, and bounce back like a champ!

Forgiving isn't about wiping your memory clean of what happened. It's more about choosing not to let that bad moment stick around and bring you down. And hey, if you're feeling sad or upset, that's totally okay.

Your feelings are like your heart's way of talking to you, and they deserve to be heard! So, give yourself a nod for being brave and facing those emotions. Forgiving is all about listening to your heart, understanding what you feel, and then deciding to step forward with a lighter load.

Our last Ingredient: Compromise

Picture this: you and your buddy can't agree on what to do for your big project, or which epic movie to watch this weekend. Sounds familiar, right? That's where knowing how to compromise comes in super handy. It's like being a teamwork wizard! But here's the thing, it's got to be done just right.

When you compromise like a pro, both you and your friend will feel like you're on the same team, with your ideas getting the high-five they deserve. Sure, you might have to give a little, but guess what? You'll end up with a plan that still has you grinning. The best part? Your friendship stays solid, like a rock.

When It's Time for a Little Space, Plus a Real Talk

Hey, it's totally cool if things aren't always smooth sailing with a friend. Sometimes, taking a step back is exactly what you need.

Think about it like this: give yourself a little me-time to mull over your friendship. Ask yourself, "Do I get pumped up when we hang out, or do I kind of wish I could disappear when their text pops up?"

If you're not ready to go full 'see ya never,' hanging out in a group could be your sweet spot. It's like having your cake and eating it too – you're not totally ditching the friendship, but you're also not in that intense one-on-one zone. It's a chill way to keep the good vibes rolling without the pressure.

But here's the deal: even after giving these steps a shot, things might still feel off. And you know what? That's totally okay.

Not every friendship is meant to last forever, and that's just part of growing up and figuring things out. What's important is you're learning and growing every step of the way. So, whether it's a time-out or a group hang, you're making the best call for you, and that's what really counts!

Finding the Right Friendship Distance

So, maybe you've tried giving each other some space or hanging out just in groups, but you're feeling like you're not as tight as before. That's totally fine, too. You can still be pals, just not super close besties.

Think of it like this: You're still there to cheer each other on for the big wins – like acing that test, nailing a cool move on your skateboard, or celebrating birthdays. But maybe you're not spilling every single secret or sharing every little thought like before. And that's okay!

Sometimes, though, you've got to make the tough call and realize it might be time to go your separate ways. Remember, you've got to look out for number one – that's you! If stepping away from a friendship is what feels right, trust your gut. It's all about finding your happy place and keeping your own well-being front and center. It's not about giving up; it's about moving forward in the best way for you.

Navigating Through a Friendship Breakdown

Hey, going through a tough time with a friend can really sting. It's like losing a piece of your daily routine, and that's hard. But here's the lowdown on how to cope and bounce back stronger:

- It's Totally Normal to Feel Blue: Yep, it's okay to feel sad, bummed out, or even a bit lost. Those feelings are part of the deal, and it's cool to let them out. You're not alone in this.
- Self-Care is Your Best Friend: Now's the time to treat yourself like the VIP you are. Dive into your favorite hobbies, or just chill and watch your go-to show. And hey, hanging with other buddies who lift you up? That's like a happiness booster shot!
- Get Busy, Get Happy: Got something you've always wanted to try? Maybe it's hitting the skate park, learning to play the guitar, or mastering the art of baking the perfect cookie. This is your golden ticket to dive in. Bonus: it keeps your mind off the tough stuff.
- New Faces, New Fun: With one door closing, a bunch of new ones are ready to swing open. This is your chance to meet new folks. Who knows? Your next best friend could be just around the corner.
- Let It All Out: Chatting about what you're going through can be a game-changer. Whether it's a family member, another friend, or even a counselor, talking helps. Pick the person you feel most comfy with.
- Keep It Classy: If you bump into your former friend, a friendly nod or a simple "Hey" can go a long way. Ending things on a peaceful note means you're walking away with your head held high, feeling good about how you handled it all.

Remember, every friendship, whether it lasts or not, teaches you something cool about yourself and others.

interaction – friendship qualities checklist

I'm going to share a list of words with you. First, take a moment to reflect on what these words mean to you personally. After that, we'll revisit the list, but this time, think about how these words might apply to your friends. It's a cool way to learn a bit about yourself and then see how you view your friendships! Ready to get started?

Here's a checklist for you to think about how you are as a friend. Check off which ones feel true to you and see where you might want to grow:

1. I'm really good at keeping secrets when my friends trust me with them.
2. I make sure to listen carefully when my friends are talking to me.
3. I'm there for my friends when they need a shoulder to cry on.
4. I encourage my friends to try new things with me.
5. I'm quick to say "sorry" when I mess up.
6. I celebrate my friends' wins like they're my own.
7. I give my friends space when they need it.
8. I'm honest with my friends, even when it's hard.
9. I stand up for my friends when others aren't being kind.
10. I check in on my friends to see how they're doing.
11. I'm patient with my friends, even when we disagree.
12. I share with my friends and don't keep score.
13. I try to make my friends laugh when they're feeling down.
14. I'm kind to my friends' other friends.

15. I try to solve problems with my friends, not make more.
16. I respect my friends' opinions, even when they're different from mine.
17. I make time to hang out with my friends.
18. I'm supportive when my friends are going through tough times.
19. I encourage my friends to be themselves.
20. I try to be positive and upbeat around my friends.
21. I'm good at giving my friends compliments.
22. I work on being understanding, even when I don't get what's going on.
23. I make an effort to get to know my friends' families.
24. I remember important things about my friends, like their birthdays.
25. I always try to be trustworthy and dependable.

See how many you checked off and think about how you might want to be an even better friend!

Alright! You've just learned some super cool stuff about being an awesome friend, spotting the not-so-great ones, and sorting out any disagreements that pop up. Now you've got the tools to make your friendships stronger and more fun.

Why not give these ideas a try in real life? Start by being the kind of friend you'd want to have, and remember, every friendship adventure is a chance to learn and grow together. Go on, put these tips into action and see how great your friendships can become!

Now that you've got a handle on friendship, let's shift our focus to something that we have talked about briefly in this chapter and super important: communication.

In the next chapter, we're going to learn about upping your communication game. This isn't just about talking; it's about really connecting with friends and understanding them better. Get ready to discover tips that'll make you not just a great talker, but an amazing listener too – which is a superpower in friendships and life in general!

boosting communication skills

E ver found yourself in a spot where what you said didn't come out right, or you just couldn't find the words? Navigating communication can be tough, but it's a game-changer when you master it.

This chapter is all about turning communication into your super-power. We'll dive into how to clearly say what you mean and really understand what others are saying, too. Ready to unlock this skill? Let's go!

Before we dive into the how-to of talking and listening like a pro, let's chat about why being good at communicating is super important.

It's not just about making friends but also doing great at school and understanding your own feelings better. Here's why:

- **Making Friends:** When you're good at talking and listening, you can make friends easily. You get to share your cool stories and understand what your friends are all about.

- **Rocking School:** Being able to explain your ideas and ask questions makes learning way more fun and easier. Plus, you get to show off your smarts in discussions and writing.
- **Understanding Feelings:** Talking about how you feel helps you get along with others and sort out tricky situations without too much drama.
- **Teamwork Makes the Dream Work:** Need a hand? No sweat! When you're a communication pro, asking for help is a breeze, and working with others is like joining forces in a superhero squad.
- **Speak Up, Stand Tall:** Every time you share your ideas or stories, it's like giving your confidence a mega boost. The more you talk, the more you shine, making you feel like the main character in your own awesome adventure.
- **Rock Any Crowd:** Whether it's a classroom presentation or a chat in the park, being a smooth talker means you can handle any scene like a star.
- **Words That Wow:** Picture yourself giving speeches that make people listen or writing stories that everyone talks about. That's the power of having ace communication skills.

effective communication techniques

1. **Eyes and Ears on Deck:** When someone's talking, lock in with those eyes and ears. Make it your mission to not just hear, but really listen. Nodding your head or throwing in a "yeah" shows you're right there with them, in the conversation's groove.
2. **Dive Deeper with Questions:** When you're curious, switch on your explorer mode and ask questions that open up a whole new world. Skip the simple "yes" or "no" stuff. Instead, ask things like "What happened next?" or "How

did that make you feel?" It's like opening a treasure chest of stories and ideas!

3. **Be a Conversation Detective:** Every time you ask a question that needs more than a one-word answer, you're inviting your friends to share a piece of their adventure with you. It's like you're both on a journey, discovering cool stuff together.

4. **Walk in Their Shoes:** Imagine you're in a video game, and you can switch characters. That's what empathy is like. Try to feel what your friend feels and see things from their side of the screen.

5. **Heart-to-Heart Connection:** Remember, everyone's got their own story. When you tune into your friend's feelings, it's like building a bridge from your heart to theirs. And guess what? That's where the real friendship magic happens.

6. **Speak Your Truth, Nicely:** When you've got something to say, let it out! But remember, it's like serving a sandwich – keep it nice. Use "I" statements like "I feel" or "I think" to share your part of the story without stepping on anyone's toes.

7. **No Blame Game:** Throwing blame around is like tossing a boomerang – it only comes back to cause more trouble. Stick to talking about your feelings and what's bugging you, without pointing fingers.

8. **More Than Words:** Guess what? Your chat power isn't just in your words! Your body tells its own story. A smile, a high-five, or even the way you stand can shout louder than words.

9. **The Silent Speakers:** Keep an eye on your face and the tone of your voice. A warm smile or a gentle tone can make your words feel like a cozy blanket, while a frown or a harsh tone might send the wrong message. It's like having a secret conversation without even speaking!

10. **The Conversation Dance:** Chatting is like a dance where everyone gets a turn to shine. Listen closely when others are in the spotlight, and they'll do the same for you. It's all about give and take, making sure everyone feels like part of the groove.

11. **Patience Pays Off:** If you've got something awesome to say, hang tight! Waiting for your turn is like holding onto a surprise gift. And when it's finally your turn, unwrap your thoughts and watch everyone's eyes light up. It's worth the wait, and it keeps the conversation flowing like a smooth melody!

12. **Be a Solution Superhero:** When things get a bit knotty, put on your problem-solving cape! Listen to what everyone's saying, toss around ideas like a hot potato, and find that sweet spot where everyone nods and says, "Yeah, that works!"

13. **Make Fair Play Your Game:** Negotiation is like being the referee in a game where everyone wins. Help each other out, trade ideas, and shake hands on a plan that makes the whole team cheer.

14. **Draw It to Show It:** If words feel like they're playing hide and seek, grab some crayons and let your drawings do the talking. It's like turning your thoughts into a colorful comic.

15. **Picture Perfect Communication:** Sometimes, a picture is worth a thousand words. If chatting isn't your jam, no worries! Point to pictures, make a cool collage, or even use emojis to share your story. It's all about getting your point across in your own awesome way!

16. **Talk the Talk Everywhere:** Whether you're at home, hanging out at school, or chilling with friends, keep those conversation skills rolling. Every chat is a chance to level up your talk-game.

17. **Become a Communication Ninja:** The more you chat, the more you'll feel like a communication ninja, smooth and

confident in every conversation. It's like training in a dojo, but for talking. Before you know it, you'll be a black belt in chit-chat!

Role-playing:

- **Act It Out, Learn a Lot:** Jump into different roles and scenarios like you're the star of your own movie. It's a cool way to walk in someone else's shoes and see the world from their eyes. Plus, it's super fun!
- **Build Your Confidence on Stage:** Every time you role-play, you're not just having a blast—you're also growing your confidence. It's like practicing for the real world in a game. You'll learn to express yourself in tons of ways, ready for any scene life throws at you.

Speak Your Mind, Kindly:

- **Be Clear, Be Heard:** When you've got something to say, don't keep it locked up! Share your thoughts loud and clear, like you're the captain of your ship. But remember, being a captain means being respectful too. It's all about saying what you need in a way that's strong but friendly.
- **Say It with Heart:** Keep your words filled with kindness, like wrapping your message in a cozy blanket. That way, people listen and respect what you've got to say, because they feel the warmth in your words.

Stand Your Ground, with a Smile:

- **Stick to Your Story**: Got an idea or an opinion? Plant your feet firm like a tree and stand by it. It's your thought, your voice, and it matters. But here's the trick – keep a smile ready. Standing strong doesn't mean being stone-cold. A smile can be your shield, showing you're confident and cool, all at once.

- **Be a Friendly Force:** When you're standing your ground, think of yourself as a friendly giant. You're big on ideas and big on respect. It's like being the friendly hero everyone roots for.

listening skills and understanding others

Listening is way more awesome than you might think. Here's the why tuning in with your ears is pretty much like unlocking a superpower:

- **Unlock Secret Levels in Conversations:** Think of listening like being a detective in a video game. When you really listen, you pick up clues that help you understand your friends and family way better. It's like unlocking secret levels in conversations where you discover cool stuff you never knew before.
- **Build an All-Star Team:** Ever watched a superhero team in action? Every member knows what the others are up to. That's what listening does in real life. When you listen to your friends, you're building a super squad where everyone feels like they matter. It's teamwork at its best!
- **Level Up Your Learning:** In class, your ears are your best tool. By listening carefully, you're grabbing all those knowledge gems your teachers are dropping. It's like having a cheat code for school – the more you listen, the more you know, and the better you do. Score!
- **Become a Wizard:** Listening is like casting a spell in your friendships. When your pals see you're really listening, they know you've got their back. It makes you the friend everyone trusts and wants to hang out with. Plus, it's a

surefire way to dodge misunderstandings and keep the good times rolling.

Alright, you're clued in on why listening rocks, but how do you show someone you're really tuning in? No worries, I've got the tricks of the trade right here for you. Let's turn you into a listening legend, step by step:

1. Using Reflections to Show You're Listening:

- **Mirror, Mirror with Words:** Reflection is like your listening mirror. When someone's talking, you can gently bounce their words back to them. It's like saying, "Hey, I hear you, and your words matter." So, if your buddy says, "I had the craziest skateboarding adventure," you can nod and say, "Whoa, a skateboarding adventure? Tell me more!" It's like giving their words a high-five.
- **Spotlight on Their Words:** When you reflect what your friend says, it's like you're shining a spotlight on their words. They'll feel super noticed and will want to keep sharing. Plus, it's like giving them a thumbs-up for their awesome storytelling skills.

2. Going Full Focus Mode for Your Friend:

- **Hit Pause on Everything Else:** When your friend's sharing something, try to put all your stuff on hold. Imagine pressing the pause button on your game or your video – that's what you're doing with everything else when your friend talks.
- **No Peeking at Screens:** Give your phone a little break too. Scrolling through social media or sneaking a peek at messages can wait. Think of it as putting your phone on

'friend mode.' It's like saying, "Hey, right now, you're way more important than anything on this screen."

3. Locking in with Your Eyes and Giving Space to Talk:

- **Eye Contact is Your Superpower:** When your friend is talking, lock eyes with them (not in a staring contest way, but a friendly way). It's like telling them, "Hey, I see you, and you're the main event right now." It makes them feel super special and heard.
- **Zip It and Let Them Rip It:** If you've got a million things you want to say, just hit the pause button on your thoughts for a sec. Let your friend have the stage, and only jump in if it's like, super-duper important. Think of it as giving them the microphone at a concert – it's their time to shine.

expressing feelings and thoughts appropriately

Remember back in Chapter 3 when we chatted about how talking about your feelings can sometimes feel like climbing a super steep hill? It's totally normal if it seems a bit tough. I don't want you to stress about it. But here's the thing – getting those feelings and thoughts out in the open is super important for you.

- **No Rush, Just Flow:** It's cool if you're not ready to spill everything at once. Think of it like a video game. You don't have to leap to the final level in one go. Take it one step at a time.
- **Why It Matters:** Sharing how you feel is like letting fresh air into a stuffy room. It helps you feel lighter, and it helps your friends understand you better. It's a win-win!
- **Find Your Chill Zone First:** Before you jump into sharing, take a little time to understand your own feelings. It's like

hitting the pause button and figuring out why you're feeling a certain way. Maybe jot down your thoughts or take a quiet walk. It's all about getting the full picture of your feelings.

- **Picture a Chill Chat:** Think about having a relaxed conversation, like you're just chatting about your favorite game or movie. When you expect things to go well, it's like setting the stage for a great talk. You'll be surprised how much your vibe can shape the conversation!

- **Jump to the Good Part:** Instead of getting tangled up in what's bugging you, zip straight to what you'd love to happen. Like, "Hey, you're awesome, and I'd be super stoked if we could hang out more!" This way, you're shining a spotlight on the positive, making it easier for your friend to understand and jump in to make things even better.

Turning the Negative into Positive: The 3-Part 'I Statement'

You know, most of the time, those gnarly feelings like anger or sadness pop up because there's something you're not really digging. Like feeling invisible when your thoughts get brushed off or feeling bummed when your buddy's always too busy. When you put it like that, it can make your friend feel cornered, and that's not the vibe you're aiming for.

So, let's flip the script and turn the negatives into positives with a super cool technique called the 3-Part 'I Statement'. Here's the game plan:

- **Start with Your Feeling:** Kick things off by owning your feeling. It's all about you here. Say, "I feel..."
- **Pinpoint the Moment:** Next, zero in on what's sparking this feeling. Slide in a "when..." to set the scene.

- **Connect the Dots:** Now, bring in the big why. Link your feeling to what you're thinking about the whole situation with a "because..."
- So instead of saying, "I'm mad because you never listen to me," you can say, "I feel frustrated when I'm sharing my game strategies, and they get overlooked because I really value our teamwork and want our plans to rock."

See? It's like you're painting a clear picture of your feelings without setting off alarm bells. It's smooth, it's clear, and it invites understanding instead of defense.

interaction – active listening challenge

7-Day Active Listening Challenge

Welcome to your 7-Day Active Listening Challenge! This week, you're going to become a conversation superhero. Each day, you'll pick one chat to really tune into, using those super listening ears. Ready? Let's jump in!

Day 1: Family Focus

> **Mission:** Choose a family member to chat with. It can be during dinner, a car ride, or just chilling at home.
> **Goal:** Really listen to their story or how their day went. Nod, make eye contact, and ask a question to dig deeper.
> **Reflection:** Write down one new thing you learned about them. Did focusing change the vibe of the talk?

Day 2: Friend File

Mission: Pick a friend to listen to. Maybe during recess, a break, or a quick call after school.
Goal: Give them your full attention. No phone checking! Show you're listening with a smile or a laugh at their jokes.
Reflection: Note down how the conversation went. Did they share more than usual because you were all ears?

Day 3: Teacher Talk

Mission: Listen actively to your teacher. Not just in class, but maybe when they're giving advice or telling a story.
Goal: Show you're interested. Nod, and maybe after class, mention something they said that you found cool.
Reflection: How did focusing on their words change your view of the class or the teacher?

Day 4: Sibling Session

Mission: If you have a brother or sister, make your chat with them today's listening mission.
Goal: Even if you chat all the time, today, really tune in. Show you're interested in what's up with them.
Reflection: Did you discover anything new? Did they seem to appreciate your attention?

Day 5: Stranger Story

Mission: Strike up a convo with someone you don't usually talk to that much. Maybe a classmate you haven't chatted with before.
Goal: Get to know something about them. Show you're genuinely interested in their story or thoughts.

Reflection: How did it feel to listen to someone new? Did it change your perspective on them?

Day 6: Mentor Moment

Mission: Find a moment to listen to someone you look up to. Could be a coach, older cousin, or family friend.
Goal: Learn one piece of advice or wisdom from them. Show you value their words by engaging and asking a follow-up question.
Reflection: What did you learn from them? How did it feel to connect on a deeper level?

Day 7: Reflection Roundup

Mission: No new conversation today. Instead, look back at your week of active listening.
Goal: Reflect on what this week taught you. How has active listening changed your conversations and relationships?
Reflection: Write down your thoughts. Are you understanding people better? Do you feel more connected?

By the end of this challenge, you'll not just be a better listener; you'll be a conversation star, making everyone around you feel heard and valued. Get ready to see some awesome changes in your chats!

Look at you! You've zoomed through Chapter 3 and 4, and now you're standing at the finish line, wearing your shiny Communication Pro badge. We've dived deep together, from mastering the art of dealing with our emotions to unlocking the secrets of top-notch talking – and heaps more!

But hey, don't just let all this cool knowledge sit there like a trophy on a shelf. It's time to take these super skills out for a spin in the real world! Every chat you have, every listen you give, every feeling you share – it's your chance to shine brighter and connect deeper.

You've totally nailed the art of talking and listening like a boss. But guess what? We've got another epic adventure waiting just around the corner. Next up, we're diving into the world of confidence. Yep, you heard it right!

In the next chapter, we're going to unlock all the secrets to feeling super sure of yourself. We'll explore cool ways to stand tall, believe in your awesome skills, and shine bright in everything you do. Imagine feeling like a superhero, no matter where you are or who you're with. That's what we're aiming for!

So, keep those pages turning, because you're about to step into the spotlight and light up the world with your newfound confidence. Get ready to feel amazing about the incredible person you are. Let's make this happen, one confident step at a time!

a word from the author

"The most important thing in communication is to hear what isn't being said."

In the introduction, I mentioned stars like Robert Downey, The Rock, and Leonardo DiCaprio. Most people would probably agree that these dudes are pretty cool … in fact, everyone wants to be around them and even be a little more like them.

I mentioned them not because of their fame but simply to reveal how easy it is to assume that people who seem to "have it together" have always been that way. I hope that by now, you have worked out the secret that not many people share with you. Nobody is born with all the skills they need to succeed. Communicating in a way that captures people's attention, being a kind and empathetic listener, working out how to solve problems … these are all abilities that anyone can hone. Yet sometimes, it seems like the places that are meant to teach you vital life lessons often miss out on sharing this vital truth.

My aim throughout this book is to show you that if you experiment with a few of these strategies and bravely commit to being the very best version of yourself, you will be unstoppable. And I hope you can help me let the cat out of the bag.

By leaving a review on Amazon, you can let other teens know that they have a superpower: the ability to reinvent themselves every day … and develop a host of useful life skills along the way.

It only takes a minute to leave a few words about how this book has helped you and why it has changed your outlook on what it means to be a happy, confident, resilient kid.

Thank you so much for your support. You could make a big difference to another kid's life.

Scan the QR code below to leave your review on Amazon.

5 /
building confidence

Have you ever had those moments where a sneaky little voice inside whispers, "Hey, you can't pull this off"? You're not alone. Everyone has that voice pop up now and then. But you know what? This is the chapter where we turn the tables on that voice. It's time to pump up the volume on how incredible, capable, and downright awesome you really are.

We're going on a journey to explore the superpowers of confidence. We'll learn how to mute that doubtful whisper. Let's get started!

understanding self-worth

Ever stumbled upon the term "self-worth" and wondered what it's all about? Well, let's break it down together. Picture self-worth as your own personal superhero, reminding you that you're a rockstar, full of potential, and totally deserving of a high-five for just being you.

Think of it this way: self-worth is like having a little meter inside you that measures how much you appreciate, love, and value yourself. It's not just about thinking you're good at this or that. It's about feeling deep down that you're worthy of all the good stuff – love, respect, and a whole lot of them!

You know how we talk about showing respect, love, and care to our buddies, family, and even our pets? Well, self-worth is all about turning that awesome care and respect inward, right back at you. It's like wearing an invisible crown that tells the world, "I've got this!" and like being your own best friend, cheering squad, and superhero, all rolled into one.

But if your self-worth feels a bit wobbly, it can be like walking around with your shoelaces tied together. You might catch yourself being super hard on yourself, zooming in on the oops moments and forgetting all about your awesome moves and skills.

Boosting your self-worth is mega important because it touches everything in your life. From the way you vibe with friends, to how you tackle your schoolwork, to that inner chat you have about yourself – it all gets a sprinkle of awesomeness when your self-worth is in superhero mode. Plus, when you see yourself as the champion you are, others will too. It's like setting the stage for some epic adventures in life.

Curious about where your self-esteem is these days? No worries, I've got a quick and super easy way for you to get a sneak peek. Just grab a comfy spot, and let's have a little heart-to-heart with these questions. Ready?

- **Your Personal High-Five Meter:** Think about how much you actually dig yourself. Do you give yourself a thumbs up, a high-five, or are you kind of shrugging? How much do you like, respect, and give a gold star to yourself?
- **Introducing You to the World:** Imagine you're meeting someone new. Which words would pop into your mind if you had to describe yourself to them? Are they like shiny trophies or more like those socks you lost under the bed?

- **Mirror, Mirror in Your Mind:** When you're chilling and your thoughts turn to you, what's the vibe? Is it like a happy playlist, a bit of a mixed tape, or more like a track that needs a serious remix?
- **You, the VIP:** Here's a big one. When you think about it, do you feel like you deserve a high-five, a pat on the back, or even a standing ovation from others?

Asking yourself these questions isn't just about getting answers. It's about starting a chat with yourself, getting to know you better, and maybe finding a few things you want to jazz up. And guess what? Just by asking, you're already on your way to boosting that self-esteem sky-high!

If the answers you just gave left you feeling a bit like you're stuck in a superhero's training montage, don't sweat it! Think of this chapter as your personal utility belt, packed with all the gadgets and technology you need to lift your self-esteem and confidence to skyscraper heights.

So, get ready to suit up, because by the time you turn the last page, you'll be more than ready to face any challenge head-on!

Ready for a bit of a brain teaser about self-worth? It's kind of like a secret garden – it's all about how you see yourself, not how everyone else sees you. Confused? No worries let's clear things up with some cool examples to power-up your understanding of self-worth.

Imagine this: There's a star athlete, let's call her Alex. She's the one everyone cheers for, the one with trophies lining her shelves. Coaches, teammates, even her family can't stop talking about her awesome skills. But here's the twist: If Alex only sees her value when she's scoring goals or winning races, what happens when she has an off day or, ouch, gets an injury? If her confidence is all about the game, it might take a nosedive whenever she's not on top of the scoreboard. Her self-worth, it turns out, is doing a tricky balancing act on her sports achievements.

Let's talk about Jake, the class comedian. He's the guy with a joke always up his sleeve, turning the whole room into a laugh riot. Everyone thinks he's the guy who's got it all together because, hey, he's always the life of the party, right?

But here's the secret twist: Jake might actually be using his super-power of humor as a shield. Behind those chuckles and giggles, he might be wrestling with some tricky thoughts, wondering if he's really as cool as people think. Even though he's the one making everyone's day brighter, deep down, he might be feeling a bit like a shadow in a very sunny room.

Now, picture Casey, the straight-A student. In everyone's eyes, she's the brainiac, the one who's got it all figured out. But if Casey's feeling like a superstar only when those A's keep rolling in, guess what happens when a tough test throws a B her way? Despite everyone's high-fives and praises, her self-worth might feel like a house of cards, shaky and ready to collapse with one unexpected grade.

See, both Alex, Jake and Casey are learning that self-worth isn't just about what you're good at or what others see. It's about knowing you're awesome, regardless of the scores, grades, or applause.

overcoming self-doubt

Now that you know what self-worth is and how it can play hide and seek with your feelings, it's time to tackle that pesky, nagging voice inside called self-doubt. You know, the one that sometimes whispers not-so-great stuff? Let's roll up our sleeves and learn some cool tricks to turn that voice from a party pooper into your personal cheerleader!

1. Spotting Sneaky Mind Tricks: How to Handle Them

Alright, let's tackle this head-on. Your mind is like a magician, sometimes pulling out tricks and illusions that aren't really true. These little mind tricks can make you see things in a not-so-great light. But guess what? Once you spot these tricks, you've got the power to flip the script. Here are four common mind tricks that your mind plays and how to catch them:

- **Black and White Thinking**: Life's not just black or white; it's a whole rainbow! So, if you catch yourself thinking it's either perfect or a disaster, remember, there's a whole range of okay-ness in between. Life's a mix, and that's what makes it cool.
- **Personalizing:** Hey, not everything's about you, and that's actually a good thing! If someone's not all smiles, it doesn't mean you're the reason. They might just be having a rough day. It's like everyone's got their own story, and you're not the villain in theirs.
- **Filter Thinking**: Imagine wearing glasses that only show you the gloomy stuff. That's filter thinking. But guess what? You can take those glasses off! Try to spot the sunshine in situations, not just the rain.
- **Catastrophizing:** This is when your mind jumps to the worst movie ending, ever. But here's a secret: you're the director of your own thoughts. So, when you feel like everything's going to go mega-wrong, grab that director's chair and remind yourself that you're in charge of the script.

2. Tackling Negative Thoughts Like a Pro

Whenever those sneaky negative thoughts try to crash your party, hit the brakes and give them a reality check. Imagine if your buddy was saying those things about themselves. You'd jump in with a superhero-sized "No way!" and show them the brighter side, right? Time to be that superhero for your own thoughts.

Ask yourself, "Am I jumping to the gloomiest conclusion, or am I being super hard on myself for no reason?" Then, switch on your detective mode and look for clues of other, happier endings or reasons why things didn't go as planned. It's like choosing your own adventure in your mind and opting for the path with sunshine and high-fives.

3. Pressing Pause on the Negative Noise

Negative thoughts can be clingy, but guess what? You can totally put them in a timeout. Imagine you're the boss of your brain, and you decide when it's time for a thought to take a little break. Give yourself a few minutes, like five, to really be with that thought. Then, when time's up, drop it like it's hot and strut into the rest of your day.

It's like your thoughts are on a playground swing. You can let them swing back and forth for a bit, but when the timer dings, it's time to hop off and go play somewhere else in the sunshine of your day. Ready to take the reins and lead your thoughts on a joy ride? Let's do this!

4. Letting Go of the Judgy Glasses

We all have those judgy glasses we put on sometimes, peaking at ourselves or others through a lens that's not too kind. But guess what? When you manage to kick those glasses off (and it's totally doable), you'll feel way more chill and comfier in your own skin.

When you catch yourself judging, just pause, check out your thoughts like you're watching clouds float by, and then let them drift away. And here's a nifty trick: flip the script and find something positive. If you find yourself going all judgey, try to spot a gold star or a high-five in the person, yourself, or the situation.

5. High-Fiving Your Life with Gratitude

Did you know saying "thanks" to life can make you feel like a million bucks? It's true! Studies show that feeling grateful can seriously up your happiness game. Even when life throws you a curveball, there's always something, even teeny-tiny stuff, that you can high-five about.

Spotting the cool things that make you smile or feel all warm and fuzzy keeps you connected to the good stuff. How about starting a gratitude journal? Just like we talked about in the previous chapters. Each day, write down a couple of things that made you feel thankful. It's like collecting happiness in a book, and on not-so-sunny days, you can flip through it and remind yourself of all the awesome things in your life.

6. Shining a Spotlight on What Makes You Awesome

Let's face it, it's super easy to get caught in a loop of oops moments and forget all the epic stuff about you. But here's a secret: shifting the spotlight to your superpowers, the things you totally rock at, can really amp up the feel-good vibes about yourself and the journey you're on. Whenever you find yourself in a tangle of not-so-nice thoughts, hit the pause button and think of something that makes you, well, you! Maybe it's your killer soccer skills, your knack for making people laugh, or how you always nail those science experiments.

7. Your Path, Your Pace: Skip the Comparison Race

Ever catch yourself stacking your chapter up against someone else's? It's like trying to play your own tune on someone else's playlist – it just doesn't mix well. Remember, life's not a race or a competition. Your buddy, your cousin, or that celeb on TV – they're jamming to their own beat, and so are you. When self-doubt tries to sneak in because someone else seems to be on a roll, turn up the volume on your own highlights. Your journey's about your own wins, big or small, and that's what makes it an epic adventure. So, keep your eyes on your own path, and let your unique awesomeness shine!

8. Power-Up with a Cheer Squad

Hanging with folks who throw shade instead of sunshine? That's like trying to fly with an anchor tied to your feet – it's a no-go for your mojo. Not everyone's going to be your cheerleader, and that's okay. But here's the deal: surround yourself with people who high-five your wins, give you a boost when you're feeling low, and genuinely dig your vibe. They're the ones who make your journey brighter and help you find your smile even on the cloudy days. So, invest your time in your personal cheer squad – the ones who make your world a whole lot sunnier.

9. Teaming Up with a Pro When the Going Gets Tough

Hey, sometimes the thoughts in our heads can get a bit too loud or tricky to handle solo. If you feel like you're stuck in a thought maze and it's getting in the way of your everyday awesomeness or snatching away the fun from your days, it's totally okay to tag in a pro. Talking to a counselor or therapist is like having a guide in your corner when life throws curveballs, helping you ease the tough stuff and growing into an even more awesome version of you. It's not just about sorting through the foggy bits; it's about discovering new paths to feeling great and making the most of this wild ride called life!

10. Energiser Mirror

Picture this: You goofed up in a game or made a whoopsie in class, and that old "Oh no, not again! I'm such a klutz!" thought starts knocking. Hold up! Instead of letting that old tune play, switch it up. Tell yourself, "Alright, that was a twist, but hey, tomorrow's a fresh start, and I've just leveled up with what I learned today."

For extra boost you can try this positive talk right after you wake up and right before you go to bed in front of a mirror.

When you make this positive self-talk your daily jam, check out the cool stuff it can do:

- **Chill Out the Stress:** It's like having a super shield that keeps stress and worry monsters at bay.
- **Boost Your Happy Meter:** Positive talk is like sunshine for your mood, making the happy vibes flow.
- **Cheer On Healthy Choices:** It's like your inner coach, pushing you to make moves that keep you fit and fine.
- **Pump Up Your Confidence:** Chat positively with yourself, and watch your confidence soar like a rocket.
- **Kick Negativity to the Curb:** Positive self-talk is like a broom, sweeping away those gloomy thoughts and keeping your mind's house sparkly clean.

Well, let's see an example of what we can say to ourselves:

1. "I am enough."
2. "I am happy."
3. "I am confident."

4. "I am strong."
5. "I am capable."
6. "I am worthy."
7. "I am loved."
8. "I am resilient."
9. "I am successful."
10. "I am at peace."

Wisdom from the Wise

Check out what these super-smart folks had to say about kicking self-doubt to the curb and believing in your own awesome self:

Sylvia Plath: "The worst enemy to creativity is self-doubt."

William Shakespeare: "Our doubts are traitors and make us lose the good we might oft win by fearing to attempt."

Toni Sorenson: "The first and most important person you must believe in is yourself."

setting and achieving personal goals

Ever thought about setting goals to supercharge your confidence? It's like putting together your own personal roadmap to awesomeness. Here's the lowdown on how setting and smashing your goals can send your confidence levels soaring.

Think of setting goals as planting your very own victory garden. Each goal is like a seed you plant. Some might be quick little sprouts, like acing a quiz, and others might be more like mighty oak trees, like becoming captain of the soccer team. Now let's see how we can set some realistic and achievable goals!

Wonder how the top players set goals they actually score? They use a cool trick called the SMART goal-setting method. It's like having a secret recipe for success. Let's break it down so you can start setting your own winning goals.

SMART is a snazzy acronym that stands for:

- **S**pecific
- **M**easurable
- **A**ttainable
- **R**elevant
- **T**ime-Bound

Alright, now let's zoom in and explore each piece of the puzzle in more detail.

SPECIFIC: *Pinning Down Your Goal*

Let's get crystal clear on your goal, making it as sharp as a snap-shot. You've got a way better shot at nailing your target if it's well-defined, not just a fuzzy wish. Instead of saying, "I want to rock my grades," how about saying, "I'm aiming for an A in math and a B in science"?

To make your goal super specific, think of it like filling out the coolest questionnaire ever. Check out these questions to help you sketch out your masterpiece of a goal:

- **What's My Victory Look Like?** Paint a picture of what you're chasing after. Is it a trophy in a competition, mastering a new skill, or acing a test?
- **Why Am I on This Quest?** Dig into the heart of your mission. Why is this goal important to your story?

- **Who's Joining My Adventure?** Think about who's part of your crew. Friends, teachers, or family – who's in on this quest with you?
- **Where's the Action?** Identify where you'll be making your moves. Is it at school, on the sports field, or maybe at home?
- **When's Showtime?** Mark your calendar for your moment of triumph. When do you plan to hit your goal?
- **What's in My Toolkit?** List what you'll need to make it happen. Books, gear, advice – what are your must-haves?
- **Any Dragons to Slay?** Spot any challenges or obstacles upfront. Knowing what you're up against is half the battle won!

By answering these questions, you're not just setting a goal; you're drawing a treasure map that leads straight to success.

MEASURABLE: Tracking Your Triumphs

Turning your goal into something you can measure is like setting up checkpoints in a game. It's about knowing exactly how far you've come and how close you are to your big win. It's the part where you add numbers or clear signs to your goal so you can see your progress and keep your motivation engine revving.

To make sure your goal is something you can track and measure, think about adding some numbers to the mix. Here are some questions to help you set those measurable markers:

- **How Much?** If it's about improving your running time, how many minutes are you aiming to shave off?
- **How Many?** If you're looking to read more books, how many books do you want to read each month?

- **How Will I Know It's Game Over?** What's the sign that'll tell you, "Yep, I did it!"? Is it a score on a test, a finished project, or something else?

By answering these, you're turning your goal into a scoreboard where every step forward counts.

ATTAINABLE: Can You Accomplish This Goal?

Setting goals is like reaching for the stars — you want to stretch out, step out of your comfort zone, and challenge yourself. But here's the kicker: you've got to keep it real. Your goals should be like a stretch that feels good — challenging, yet something you can actually achieve. It's all about finding that sweet spot where you're willing to hustle but can realistically see yourself crossing the finish line.

Take, for example, your dream of joining the varsity soccer team. Imagine you're just starting high school, fresh-faced and eager. There's a catch, though — the coach has a rule about not letting first-years into the varsity team. It might feel like a bummer, but here's a thought: why not aim for the junior varsity team instead? It's a solid stepping stone. You get to show what you're made of, gain valuable experience, and set yourself up for success. Then, come sophomore year (or junior or senior, no rush!), making varsity will be more than just a dream; it'll be a goal you're ready to achieve.

So, let's break it down:

- **Challenge Yourself:** Step out of your comfort zone and aim high.
- **Keep It Real:** Make sure your goals are something you can actually see yourself achieving.

- **Plan Ahead:** If the direct route isn't available, find a stepping stone that will lead you to your ultimate goal.

By keeping it real and planning smart, you're not just dreaming; you're on your way to making those dreams come true.

RELEVANT: Is Your Goal Constructive?

Let's talk about making your goal count. It's all about focusing on the endgame, not just keeping busy. Your goal should be a stepping stone to leveling up, whether it's boosting your brainpower or growing personally.

Think of it this way: every goal should be a power-up, propelling you forward. And by keeping your eyes on the prize, you'll make sure every step you take is one step closer to where you want to be.

TIME-BOUND: Set a Deadline to Make It Happen

Deadlines aren't just for homework. When it comes to your goals, setting a "due date" is crucial. Without a finish line, where's the rush? There's a magic in deadlines that turns "someday" into "let's do this!"

Since you're juggling your goals with school life, why not use semesters and school years as your timeline? They're perfect checkpoints to assess how far you've come and how far you've got to go.

So, let's break it down:

- **Focus On Results**: Make sure your goal isn't just busy work. Aim for something that levels you up.
- **Set a Deadline:** Choose a realistic timeframe to turn "I wish" into "I will."

By focusing on what really matters and setting a clear timeline, you're not just setting goals—you're setting yourself up for success. And don't forget along with SMART you should also plan your day, week and month!

interaction - positive affirmation cards

Hey there! Ready to create your very own superhero cards? Not just any cards, but positive affirmation cards (just like the ones we mentioned in this chapter!) that are like your personal cheerleaders, rooting for you every day. These aren't just words on paper; they're your secret weapon to feeling awesome, confident, and ready to take on the world. Let's dive in on how to make these magic cards!

Step 1: Grab Some Supplies

First up, you'll need some cardstock or thick paper, markers, stickers — whatever gets your creative juices flowing. This is your project, so make it as colorful and cool as you like.

Step 2: Think It, Believe It, Write It

Now, let's talk affirmations. These are super positive statements that help you believe in yourself. The trick is to write them as if they're already true. Instead of saying, "I will be successful," you say, "I am successful." Instead of "I will be happy," you say, "I am happy." See the difference? It's like you're telling your brain, "Hey, this is happening right now!"

Step 3: Make It Personal and Powerful

Your affirmations should be about you and for you. Think about what makes you feel good or what you want to believe about yourself. Here are some examples to get you started:

- "I am brave and tackle challenges head-on."
- "I am a great friend who listens and supports."
- "I am smart and learn from every experience."

Step 4: Decorate Your Cards

This is where the fun really starts! Decorate each card with drawings, stickers, or anything that makes you smile. Each card should feel like a mini celebration of who you are.

Step 5: Use Them Daily

Keep your cards somewhere you'll see them often, like on your desk, by your bed, or in your backpack. Every morning, pick a card or two and read them out loud. It's like giving your brain a pep talk before you start your day.

Remember, the more you believe in your affirmations, the more powerful they become. It's not just about saying the words; it's about feeling them in your heart and believing them with all you've got.

Creating positive affirmation cards is like building your own team of superheroes, always there to remind you of your strengths, dreams, and how incredibly awesome you are. So, what are you waiting for? Let's get crafting and create those positive vibes!

interaction - goal-setting worksheet

Name _____ Goal Setting

SMART Goal Setting

In as few words as possible, write down your goal.

My goal is to: _____

Make your goal specific. What actions will you take to achieve this goal?

1. _____

2. _____

3. _____

Make your goal measurable. How will you track your progress? How will you know you have reached your goal?

I will use the following numbers or methods to measure my progress: _____

_____

I will know I have reached my goal when: _____

_____

Make your goal attainable. I need the following things to achieve my goal:

_____

How I will find the time to work on my goal: _____

_____

I need to educate myself about: _____

I will get support from: _____

Make your goal relevant. Why is it important for you to achieve this goal?

Make your date time bound.

I will reach my goal by: _____ I will get halfway to my goal by: _____

Additional milestones: _____

In this chapter, we've embarked on an epic journey through the realms of self-worth and confidence, uncovering the superpowers that lie within you. And now, armed with the knowledge and tools from the SMART system, you're more than ready to turn your dreams into reality. Remember, with SMART goals—Specific, Measurable, Attainable, Relevant, and Time-bound—the sky's the limit! Each step you've learned is like a piece of your armor, designed to make you unstoppable in your quest. So, hold your head high, believe in your incredible abilities, and let's make those goals happen.

Feeling that boost of confidence already? Awesome! But hey, that's just the beginning. Up next, we're diving into something super important and cool: mental resilience. Ever wonder how to spring back from those oh-no moments and keep charging ahead? Well, you're about to become a pro at it. Mental resilience is your secret weapon for facing challenges head-on and not just surviving but thriving. Ready to level up your game and become even more unstoppable? Buckle up, because we're just getting started. Let's jump into the next adventure together!

6 /
mental resilience

E ver had one of those days where it feels like everything's against you, and you just want to throw in the towel? Yeah, we've all been there. But imagine this: what if, instead of giving up, you could come back even stronger every single time life decides to toss a curveball your way? Sounds pretty cool, right? This chapter's mission is to help you craft your very own mental armor. That's right, we're talking about becoming a resilience ninja, ready to tackle any challenge that comes your way. So, are you ready to learn the secrets to bouncing back better than ever? Let's dive in and get started!

coping with stress and anxiety

Alright, let's chat about something called anxiety. You know how sometimes you think or feel something that seems super scary? That's what anxiety is like. But here's the cool part: even though it feels intense, anxiety isn't something that can actually harm you. In fact, believe it or not, it can sometimes be like a superhero signal like spidey-senses in your body, telling you to be careful or get ready for something important.

So, here are a few key points to keep in mind about anxiety:

- **Anxiety is like a warning signal:** It can pop up as thoughts in your mind or feelings in your body that make you feel uneasy or scared.
- **Anxiety is not a bad guy:** It might feel uncomfortable, but it's not dangerous. It's actually trying to help you in its own way.
- **Everyone feels it:** Yup, you heard that right. Every single person experiences anxiety at some point. It's totally normal.

But what if someone feels scared a lot, about lots of things, and it starts getting in the way of having fun, doing well in school, or hanging out with friends and family? That's when it might be something called an anxiety disorder.

Here's a quick look at what that could mean with some examples:

- **Separation Anxiety:** Feeling super scared about being away from mom or dad.
- **Phobias:** Being really, really scared of specific things or situations, like dogs, bugs, or visiting the doctor.
- **Social Anxiety:** Feeling extremely shy or scared around other people or when you need to speak up in class.
- **General Anxiety:** Worrying a lot about what might happen in the future, like thinking about all the "what ifs."
- **Panic Disorder:** Having sudden moments where you feel really terrified, your heart beats super-fast, you might find it hard to breathe, or you feel dizzy or shaky.

Anxiety isn't just about feeling scared or worried; it can make someone feel cranky or angry, have trouble sleeping, or even feel tired all the time, get headaches, or have a tummy ache. Sometimes, kids don't talk about these worries, so it's not always easy to see what's going on.

Remember, everyone feels anxious now and then, but if it's happening a lot and messing with day-to-day stuff, it's important to chat about it with someone who can help, like a parent, teacher, or counselor.

I can almost hear you asking, 'So, what can we do if we're feeling this way?' Great question! Here are some simple steps you can start doing today to help manage those tricky feelings:

1. Belly Breathing: The Superhero Relaxation Technique

Ever noticed how when you're super nervous or stressed, your breathing goes all fast, your heart starts racing, and your muscles feel like they've turned into rocks? Yeah, not a great feeling, because it makes it super hard to think straight. But guess what? There's a cool trick to help with that, and it's called belly breathing. It's like a secret power for calming down anxiety and even helping with pain.

How to Become a Belly Breathing Pro:

- **Find Your Spot:** Get comfy lying down or sitting in a chair with your feet flat on the ground.
- **Hand Positions:** Place one hand on your belly and the other on your chest. This is your control panel.
- **Deep Dive:** Take a big breath in through your nose and imagine filling your lungs with air like you're inflating a balloon inside your belly. The hand on your belly should rise, but the one on your chest should pretty much stay put.
- **The Big O:** As you breathe out, make your lips into an "O" and blow out all that air. Feel your belly go down and your muscles get a mini workout as they tighten.

- **Repeat Mode:** Keep going with this belly breathing magic. It's your go-to move when you need a moment of peace or when something hurts.

Like any superhero skill, the more you practice belly breathing, the stronger it gets. And the best part? Everyone in the family can join in, no matter how old they are.

2. Move It to Improve It: Fun Ways to Get Active

Did you know that moving around and getting your heart pumping isn't just awesome for your body, but it's also super good for your brain and mood? That's right! Whether you're feeling bored, a bit sluggish, super energetic, sad, grumpy, or jittery, shaking things up with some activity is like hitting the reset button on your emotions.

And guess what? You don't need a bunch of fancy equipment or heaps of time to get moving. All you need is a little creativity and the willingness to have fun. If you have any health concerns, make sure to have a quick chat with your doctor to see what activities are good to go. Once you've got the thumbs up, the sky's the limit!

Ideas to Kickstart Your Active Adventures:

- Take a family expedition around the neighborhood.
- Zoom around on a tricycle or bike.
- Tidy up and rearrange your space for a mini-workout.
- Create an epic outdoor adventure with your imagination.
- Play fetch with your furry family member.
- Dive into swimming fun.
- Shake it up with a kid-friendly workout video.
- Dance your heart out to your favorite songs.
- Get the gang together for some lively games.
- Master the art of jump roping.

- Toss a ball or shoot hoops.
- Hitting the pavement for a run.
- Pumping iron at the gym (don't forget a spotter!).
- Unwinding with a yoga session at home or in a class.
- Getting fit with online workout videos.
- Exploring on a bike ride.
- Gliding on rollerblades.
- Joining a team sport or playing casual games with pals.
- Trekking through nature on a walk or hike.
- Moving to the beat in a dance class.

Let these suggestions spark your imagination and guide you to activities that make getting active a blast. The goal here is to mix things up, try something new, or stick with what you love. Either way, let's get moving and have a ton of fun!

3. Guided Imagery: Your Imagination's Superpower

Ever pretended you're chilling on a sunny beach to forget about a stressful day? Well, that's not just make-believe; it's a real-deal way to help your brain take a mini-vacation from stress. This awesome trick is called guided imagery.

How to Dive into Guided Imagery:

Guided imagery lets kids and teens (yeah, you!) use their super-power of imagination to switch up how they're feeling. It's like daydreaming on purpose, where you get to create a fun adventure in your mind.

Follow these steps to become a guided imagery master:

- **Find Inspiration:** Look at pictures or videos of a place you love, or think of a happy memory, a yummy smell, or anything that makes you smile.
- **Set the Scene:** If you've got a photo or video, check it out first. If not, no worries—just close your eyes and let the magic begin.
- **Pick Your Paradise:** Imagine you're in your happy place. It could be anywhere: a beach, a park, grandma's kitchen—any spot where you feel super happy and safe.
- **Detail Detective**: Use your daydreaming skills to explore every little thing about your special place. What do you see? What scents are in the air? What can you taste and hear? How does the ground feel beneath you?
- **Scent-sational:** If there's a smell you love or one that reminds you of this place, bring it into your adventure. It can make your imaginary visit even more relaxing.
- **Body Check:** Notice how awesome and comfy you feel while exploring your happy place. Your breathing might slow down, and your muscles might feel like they're melting—totally relaxed.
- **Back to Reality:** When you're ready, and you've soaked up all the good vibes, open your eyes.

Sometimes, it might be tricky to do this on your own. If that happens, no problem! Ask someone to help by describing a peaceful place while you listen with your eyes closed.

Guided imagery is like a secret getaway, anytime, anywhere. So, whenever you need a break or a blast of happiness, just close your eyes and let your imagination do the walking!

4. Journaling: Your Personal Adventure Book

A journal is like your own secret diary, but way cooler. It's a special place where kids and teens can spill their thoughts, feelings, and what's happening in their lives. Think of it as your brain's best friend, where you can let out all your stress, celebrate the awesome stuff, work through tough emotions, and even solve some mysteries about yourself. Whether you're feeling down, pumped up, or just plain curious, your journal is there for you, no judgment!

Kicking Off Your Journaling Journey:

First, snag a notebook and a pen. Old school pen and paper are perfect for this, but if you're more of a tech whiz, tapping away on a tablet or computer is cool too. Find a cozy, quiet spot where you can chill without anyone bugging you.

Now, it's time to let your words flow. Don't sweat about doing it "right." There's no such thing in journaling. If you're stuck on what to write, here are some epic ideas to start with:

- Recap what you did today.
- Chat about something you're super excited for and why.
- Share what's been bugging you lately and why.
- Remember a moment you felt like a superhero or super proud.
- Think about something you'd change if you had a magic wand.

Your journal is your private treasure chest, but if you ever feel like sharing a page or two with someone else, that's cool too. Starting with just 10 minutes of journaling can be a great way to begin. The more you do it, the more you'll discover about yourself, and the better you'll feel about... well, everything!

So, grab that notebook just like we have talked about on the previous chapters and start your journaling adventure. Who knows what amazing stories you'll tell?

5. The Power of Saying Thanks

Who says you have to wait for Thanksgiving to count your blessings? Giving thanks is like a superpower you can use any time of the day to boost your mood and feel awesome. Whether you're having a great day or one of those where everything seems to go wrong, taking a moment to remember the good stuff can really turn things around.

It's not just about feeling better when you're down or grumpy; it's also about keeping track of the amazing things in your life, big or small. Here's how you can make giving thanks a fun part of your daily routine:

Gratitude Journaling:

Grab a notebook and turn it into your gratitude journal. Think about all the things you're thankful for—your family, friends, a cozy home, cool experiences, or even your favorite ice cream flavor. You can write them down, doodle, or stick in some fun stuff like photos or stickers.

More Fun Ways to Practice Gratitude:

- **Write a Thank-You Letter:** Pen a letter to someone special, telling them why you're grateful for them. You can mail it, read it to them in person, or even share it over a call.
- **Three Cheers for Today:** Each day, jot down three awesome things that happened. Maybe you aced a quiz, made a new buddy, or had a really good laugh.

- **The Story Behind the Good Stuff:** Don't just list the good things—think about why they happened. Did you make a new friend because you were brave and said hi first? Did that A+ come from your love for the subject or because you put in the study hours?
- **Send Some Love:** Write down all the good vibes and wishes you have for someone and give it to them. Try this for someone close, like a family member, and then for a friend or someone you don't see as often.

Making gratitude a part of your day is like giving your brain a happiness boost. So why wait? Start today and watch how it helps melt stress away and brings in loads of happy vibes!

6. Chill-Out Moves: Muscle Relaxation Magic

Ever felt so nervous, stressed, or upset that your body feels all tight and uncomfortable? There's a superhero move for that, and it's called muscle relaxation. It's like a game where you tense up your muscles on purpose and then let them relax. This trick is awesome because it helps your brain focus on just one thing at a time and teaches you how to notice when you're feeling tense and how to let that tension go.

Let's Get Started with Muscle Relaxation:

First, find a cozy spot where you can either lie down or sit comfortably with your feet flat on the ground. Kick things off with five to 10 big belly breaths to get into relaxation mode.

Now, let's go on a muscle-tensing and relaxing adventure:

- **Face Time:** Scrunch up all the muscles in your face—think eyes, nose, cheeks, and forehead. Imagine you're trying to make a raisin face. Hold it tight, count to 10, and then—whoosh—let it all melt away.

- **Jaw Power:** Pretend you've got a giant jawbreaker in your mouth and clench your teeth. Hold it for a superhero count of 10 and then release. Feel that tension drop away.
- **Shoulder Shrug:** Lift those shoulders up like you're a turtle hiding in its shell. Squeeze... and let go. Repeat a couple of times, and don't forget to keep breathing those belly breaths.
- **Back Stretch:** Arch your back, trying to make your shoulder blades touch (they won't, but it's fun to try!). Hold, then let go and relax.
- **Rocky Stomach:** Suck in your tummy, making it as hard as a rock. Hold for three seconds, then release and let it go soft.
- **Arm Lift:** Stretch your arms up high, reaching for the stars, then let them fall back down. Or hug yourself tight, squeeze, and release.
- **Fist Squeeze:** Make tight fists, like you're trying to squeeze all the juice out of a giant lemon, then let go and shake them out.
- **Legs and Toes:** Tense up those legs, curl your toes under like you're trying to grab something with them, and then let it all go. Imagine your legs feeling super warm and relaxed.

After you've worked through each part of your body, take a few more of those big, calming belly breaths. Enjoy that awesome feeling of being totally relaxed.

7. Kindness Boomerang: How to Pay It Forward

Ever heard of the saying, 'What goes around, comes around'? Well, 'paying it forward' is kind of like that, but with kindness. It means doing something nice for someone else, just because. The cool part?

When you do good things, you end up feeling pretty great too! So, if you're feeling down, lonely, or even a bit grumpy, or you see someone else who could use a smile, why not try paying it forward?

Kindness Mission: Your Pay It Forward Plan

Grab some paper and a pen (or a pencil), and let's brainstorm. First up, think of people or even pets who might need a little boost. Then, let's figure out some awesome ways you can make their day brighter. Here are some ideas to get you started:

- **Story Time:** Read your favorite book to a younger sibling, cousin, or buddy.
- **Food Hero:** Donate some yummy food to a local food bank.
- **Eco-Warrior:** Clean up trash in your neighborhood or at a park.
- **Animal Buddy:** Spend some time helping out at an animal shelter.
- **Green Thumb:** Offer to help with gardening or yard work for family or neighbors.
- **Super Sitter:** If you're old enough, offer to babysit for free to give someone a well-deserved break.
- **Snack Squad:** Bring a snack or treat to someone feeling under the weather.
- **Compliment Club:** Make someone's day with a genuine compliment.
- **Card Creators:** Craft a card for kids in a hospital or your classmates just because.

Soon enough, you'll notice that spreading kindness not only makes others happy but gives you a major happiness boost too.

Let's dive into some super cool books that tackle something we all feel. These stories are all about showing us we're not alone in this and teaching us some awesome ways to handle those jittery feelings.

Wemberly Worried by Kevin Henkes: Imagine being a tiny mouse with big worries, especially about starting school for the first time. That's Wemberly for you! This book is a sweet ride into understanding that it's okay to feel anxious and that talking about our worries can make them feel a lot less scary.

Help Your Dragon Deal with Anxiety by Steve Herman: Picture this: you've got a dragon (yes, a dragon!) and it's feeling all kinds of nervous. This story is a fun adventure that teaches us cool tricks to calm down anxiety, not just for dragons, but for kids too!

David and the Worry Beast by Anne Marie Guanci: Meet David and his not-so-friendly beast that grows bigger with every worry. Through David's journey, we learn that we have the power to shrink our worries down to size. It's a great way to see how facing our fears can actually make them a lot less beastly.

These books are like secret guides to dealing with worry, showing us that with a little courage and some new skills, we can tackle anything that makes us feel anxious.

positive thinking and mindset

Think of positive thinking not just as seeing the sunny side of things, but as building an awesome fortress where your spirit is the brave hero, ready to face any adventure life throws at you with a smile and a can-do attitude.

Now, here's a cool fact: our brains are like supercomputers that believe whatever story we tell them. So, if you wake up and think, "Oh man, today's going to be rough," your brain starts looking for proof to make that story true. It's like having a sneaky sidekick that's always trying to match your expectations.

That's why filling your head with positive thoughts is like choosing the best sidekick for your adventures. It's super important, especially for you guys! Imagine if, instead of thinking a day, a week, or even a whole year is just a bunch of bloopers, you start seeing it as a collection of epic levels you've conquered.

By training your brain to think positively, you're not just avoiding writing off days as bad news. You're actually programming your mind to spot the awesome stuff, making every moment an opportunity to score points in the game of life.

To get better at this skill don't forget to pay extra attention to Chapter 5's: Overcoming Self-Doubt.

When you level up your mindset to boss mode with positive thinking, it's like putting on a pair of super goggles that transform how you see the world. Here's how your outlook on life gets an epic upgrade when you reach that awesome level of positivity:

Morning School Shuffle:

Feeling a Bit Blah? Mornings can be tough, especially when school's calling, and your bed's super cozy. But here's a cool way to look at it: "Okay, I might not be super pumped right now, but once I get going, things will look up. School's like my mission field, where I earn my stripes (and fun times)!"

When You're Feeling Down on Yourself:

Not Feeling Top of the Game? Remember, everyone has those moments of feeling a bit less than stellar. Flip that thought with, "Hey, I'm just as cool and capable as anyone out there. I've got what it takes, and every step I take is me backing myself up. Time to be my own biggest fan!"

Randomly Feeling Blue:

Just One of Those Days? We all get them – those days when you're just not feeling it, and you don't even know why. Here's a thought to turn it around: "Today's got the potential to be awesome, and I get to decide to make it that way. Let's do this!"

Oops, Flunked a Test:

Test Didn't Go as Planned? It feels rough, for sure. But here's a different angle: "So I stumbled a bit, but hey, I stepped up and gave it my best shot. This is just round one. With a bit of a regroup and some extra study ninja moves, I'll come back swinging for round two!"

When the Weather's Being a Party Pooper:

Gloomy Skies? Sometimes the weather decides to throw its own kind of party, and it's not the fun kind. But even then, you can say, "Alright, the sky's got the grumps today, but that doesn't mean I have to. Time to make my own sunshine!"

Remember, you've got the power to turn your thoughts around and make any day, situation, or moment a win.

dealing with failure and setbacks

Hey, did you know that every time you trip up or miss the mark, you're actually on the fast track to becoming a mega-smart, super-skilled version of yourself? Yep, it's true! Failure isn't the big, scary monster it's made out to be. It's more like a wise old coach that's here to teach you some epic life lessons.

Think of it like playing your favorite video game. Every time you face a tough level and don't quite make it, you learn a bit more about how to dodge those obstacles or tackle those tricky challenges. The next time you're at it, you've got all that know-how backing you up, ready to level up like a champ. Here are 7 steps to help you adopt this mindset:

1. Powering Up with a Growth Mindset

Do you remember this super cool thing called a growth mindset? It's the secret key that unlocks your brain's ability to learn from every single thing that happens, especially the tricky stuff like failures.

Get this: some brainy folks did a study and found out that when kids with a growth mindset slip up or make a mistake, their brains light up way more than those with fixed mindsets. It's like their brains are saying, "Hey, that didn't go as planned, but watch me learn something awesome from it!"

When things don't go your way, having a growth mindset is like being a detective at the scene. You look around, gather clues (like what went wrong and why), and then use those clues to come up with a super plan to do better next time.

Here's the deal:

- **Mistakes Are Cool:** Yep, you heard that right. Every oops moment is your brain growing and figuring out new, smarter ways to do things.
- **Be a Fix-It Wizard:** Instead of just feeling bummed about a mistake, put on your wizard hat and ask, "What spell can I

cast to fix this?" It's all about finding the magic formula that turns your "uh-oh" into a "ta-da!"

- **Learn and Level Up:** Every time you learn from a mistake, it's like you're leveling up in the game of life. You're getting stronger, smarter, and way cooler at tackling whatever challenge comes next.

2. Embracing Failure: It's Part of the Adventure

Guess what? Running into a bit of trouble or flunking something isn't just okay; it's actually part of becoming a super cool, wise, and tough version of you. I know, it sounds a bit wild, right? But even though it's super tempting for parents or grown-ups to swoop in and save the day, sometimes the bravest thing they can do is take a step back.

Jessica Lahey, who wrote this awesome book called "The Gift of Failure," tells us that when you face challenges and even slip up, your brain is busy building some seriously epic skills like problem-solving and bouncing back from tough times. If you never get the chance to face a challenge head-on, it's like missing out on some major brain workout sessions.

So, when you're in a sticky situation or about to face something that makes you a bit nervous, think about these power questions:

- **What Would a Fearless Grown-Up Do?** Imagine if the grown-ups in your life weren't scared at all. How would they let you handle this?
- **Is This Really a Mega Crisis?** Ask yourself, is this mistake something super huge, or is it something you can learn from and move past?
- **What Cool Stuff Will I Learn?** If the grown-ups take a step back and you get to tackle this, what awesome new skills or lessons might you pick up?

Giving yourself space to stumble a bit isn't about making things tough; it's about growing tougher, smarter, and more ready to take on the world. Remember, failure isn't the end of the game. It's just a twist in the plot that makes your story even more epic.

3. High-Fiving Your Way Through Failures

Who knew that those oops moments could actually be your secret ticket to becoming a genius? That's right, each mistake is like a mystery box full of learning goodies. So, why not throw a mini-party every time you trip up, knowing you've just unlocked a brand new level of smarts?

Check out these awesome ways to make every mistake feel like a win:

- **Mistake Show-and-Tell:** Got a funny or epic fail story? Share it like a badge of honor and chat about the cool stuff you figured out from it.
- **Failure Fridays:** How about dedicating one day a week to learning about legends who stumbled before they soared? It's like collecting tales of triumph to power up your own journey.
- **High-Five for Try:** Every time you give something a shot and it doesn't go as planned, how about a high-five? It's like saying, "Nice move, keep playing the game!"
- **My Favorite 'No' Time:** Spot a mistake that's actually pretty awesome because of what you can learn from it? Make it your "Favorite No" of the day and dive into what was super smart about the slip and how to ace it next time.
- **FAIL = First Attempt in Learning:** Think of FAIL as your secret code for "I just tried something cool, and I'm one step smarter because of it!"

When you start seeing each stumble as just another step on your epic adventure to awesomeness, suddenly, failures aren't scary – they're part of the fun, part of learning, and part of what makes you, well, pretty incredible.

4. Navigating the Adventure of 'The Learning Pit'

Ever heard of 'The Learning Pit'? It's a super cool way to look at those times when you feel a bit lost or stuck, like you're on a tricky level in a game. James Nottingham came up with this neat idea to help us understand that getting a bit tangled up is actually a big part of learning and growing.

Think of it like this: whenever you bump into a challenge, you're actually stepping into 'the pit.' It's a place where your brain is working overtime, sorting through the "Uh-oh, I'm stuck" or "Yikes, I goofed up" thoughts. But here's the secret – it's in 'the pit' where your brain is doing some of its best work, cooking up new ideas and figuring out smarter ways to do things.

You can make 'the pit' a regular part of your chat. When you're tackling something tough, ask yourself or your friends, "Who's hanging out in the pit right now?" or "Who's just climbed out?" It's like checking in on where everyone's at in the adventure.

In school, you can team up with your classmates, especially if someone's in 'the pit' and someone else has just climbed out. It's like joining forces – one's got the map, and the other's got the flashlight, ready to conquer the challenge together.

So, next time you find yourself in 'the pit,' remember, it's not a trap – it's part of the journey to becoming even more awesome.

5. Unlocking Brain Power: The Science of Learning from Mistakes

Did you know that every time you slip up or face a tough puzzle, your brain is actually getting a workout? Yep, it's true! There's a whole bunch of science that says making mistakes is like doing brain push-ups. Let's break it down and see how tripping up can be your ticket to becoming brainy-strong!

If You're Worried About Making a Mistake...

Think of Mistakes as Brain Sparks: Every time you goof up, it's like your brain is setting off little fireworks of learning. These sparks help your brain grow and get stronger. Cool, right? A study by some smart folks even showed that your brain lights up and grows every time you make a mistake. It's like your own brain gym!

If You're Nervous About Making a Wrong Guess...

Guessing is Your Secret Weapon: Making guesses, even wrong ones, is like having a secret key to learning. When you make a guess and then find out the right answer, it sticks in your brain like super glue. It's a bit like playing a memory game – making a wrong guess and then learning the right answer helps your brain remember it even better next time.

Challenges Make You a Brain Boss

Sure, when you're learning something really tricky, you might make more mistakes. But guess what? That just means your brain is working extra hard, and that's a good thing! The tougher the challenge, the better your brain holds onto the info. It's like lifting heavier weights to get stronger muscles – the harder you work, the stronger your brain gets!

So, next time you're facing a brain-bender or worrying about getting something wrong, just remember – it's all part of turning your brain into a mega-mind.

6. Mastering the Art of "Failing Forward"

Guess what? Every time you stumble or mess up, you're actually stepping forward, not backward. It might sound a bit wacky, but it's true! Instead of running away from mistakes, we can use them to grow and get even better. When you start asking yourself, "What did I learn from this?" or "How can I rock it next time?" you're turning oops moments into a-ha moments.

"Failing forward" is a cool trick that even big-time business folks use. It's all about picking up secret tips and tricks from every trip and tumble.

Elaine Taylor-Klaus, a pro coach and super-parent, reminds us to "fail forward into life." She knows a thing or two, especially being the parent of a kid with special needs. She tells us that making mistakes is just part of being human, and that's totally okay. We just need a little nudge to remember that it's all part of the adventure.

7. Navigating Tough Times with a Mindful Map

Even when you've got all these cool strategies up your sleeve, sometimes failures can still feel like a giant wave crashing down. That's where learning to be mindful, like a mental ninja, can really help you ride those waves like a champ.

Did you know that being mindful can make you super resilient? It's like having a secret shield against the tough stuff.

So, how can you become a mindfulness master? There's this awesome technique called RAIN, created by Michelle McDonald, and it's like having a map through the stormy weather of big emotions. Let's check out the steps:

R for Recognize: Spot what's going on inside your head. Ask yourself, "What's the weather like in my mind right now? How does my body feel about this?"

> Example: "Man, I'm really bummed about that test. Feels like there's a thunderstorm in my chest."

A for Allow: Let the feelings hang out, even if they're not the fun kind. It's like saying, "Okay, feelings, you can stay for a bit."

> Example: "I'm feeling down, and my heart's doing a sad dance. It's not fun, but it's okay to feel this way."

I for Investigate: Put on your detective hat and dig a little deeper. Ask, "Why am I feeling this? Is there more to the story?"

> Example: "Hmm, I'm not just upset; I'm also a bit let down. Maybe it's because I think I could've prepped more for that test."

N for Non-Identification: Remember, you're way more than just your feelings. It's like saying, "These feelings are just visitors; they don't define me."

> Example: "Sure, I've got a storm of feelings right now, but I'm the sky – way bigger than any weather passing through."

To give RAIN a try, you can write down these steps and go through them with something that didn't go your way. Then, if you're up for it, see if you want to navigate your feelings with this cool technique.

interaction – stress-o-meter

Ready to become a stress detective and discover some awesome ways to chill out? Let's build your very own 'Stress-O-Meter'! It's like having a dashboard that shows how revved up your engines are and gives you the best tricks to cool them down. Here's how you can set it up and match your stress levels with some cool-down tactics:

Green Zone: Feeling Chill

Stress Level: Low – You're feeling pretty good, like a calm sea or a gentle breeze.
Coping Strategies: Keep up the good vibes! Maybe listen to your favorite tunes, doodle in your notebook, or spend some time with your pet. It's all about keeping that green zone glow.

Yellow Zone: A Bit Bumpy

Stress Level: Medium – You're a little rattled, like when the waves get choppy or the wind picks up.
Coping Strategies: Time to slow down and take some deep breaths. Maybe take a walk, chat with a friend, or do something that makes you laugh. It's like finding a cozy spot to wait out the breeze.

Orange Zone: Storm's Brewing

Stress Level: High – Things are feeling pretty intense, like a storm is on the horizon.
Coping Strategies: Let's get serious about stress-busting. Try writing down what's bugging you, doing some serious phys-

ical activity, or practicing mindfulness or meditation. It's like battening down the hatches and getting ready for the storm.

Red Zone: Stress Overload

Stress Level: Super High – You're in the middle of the storm, and it's all hands on deck.
Coping Strategies: This is when you might need some backup. Talk to someone you trust – a family member, a friend, or maybe a counselor. Sometimes, just sharing what's on your mind can turn the storm into a drizzle. It's like calling in the rescue team when the seas get rough.

With your 'Stress-O-Meter' ready, you're all set to check in with yourself and pick the best moves to keep your cool, no matter what the stressful weather brings your way. Ready to navigate the waves like a stress-busting captain? Anchors aweigh!

Setting Sail with Your Stress-Busting Gear

Hey, look at you! You're now decked out with some of the coolest, most high-tech gear for tackling stress and anxiety. It's like you've got your own personal toolbox filled with gadgets and gizmos that are perfect for any situation life throws your way.

But hey, all this awesome gear isn't just for show. It's made for action! So, how about we take these tools for a spin in the real world? Whether it's trying out your 'Stress-O-Meter' on a hectic day or turning a tough moment into a learning adventure with the RAIN technique, you've got what it takes to navigate through the waves and come out sailing smoothly.

Remember, every great explorer, superhero, or legendary adventurer started where you are right now. They took that first step, tried out their gear, and learned how to make it work best for them. And you can do the same!

Alright, champion! You've just powered up with some top-notch tools to boost your mental toughness and keep stress at bay. But guess what? There's another level of awesomeness waiting just around the corner, and it's all about the power of kindness and respect.

In the next chapter, we're going to dive into how being a good guy doesn't just make the world a brighter place – it turns you into a real-life superhero. We'll uncover the secrets of how leading with kindness and dishing out respect can be your ultimate superpower, making you stronger, happier, and an all-around legend.

7 /
leading with kindness and respect

Picture this: a world where every high-five, every smile, and every word is packed with kindness and respect. Sounds like the coolest place ever, doesn't it? Well, guess what? In this chapter, we're not just daydreaming about it; we're rolling up our sleeves and making it real. And it all starts with you.

Yep, you've got the power to be a leader in spreading kindness like a superhero spreading good vibes. You might be thinking, "Me? A leader?" Absolutely! You don't need a cape or a secret identity. All you need is the courage to be kind, the strength to show respect, and the willingness to make a difference, one awesome act at a time. Ready to discover how you can light up the world? Let's get started.

Before we jump into becoming the coolest, kindest leader on the block, let's hit the pause button and dig into why being kind is such a big deal. And here's a little spoiler alert: it's not just about making the day brighter for the people around you (though that's super important too).

Here's the lowdown on why leveling up your kindness is like unlocking a secret level in the game of life:

- **Building a Super Society:** Picture a place where everyone's tossing kindness around like confetti at a parade. Pretty awesome, right? That's the kind of world we're aiming for. A place where everyone's cool with each other, cares heaps, and nobody's left out just because they're a bit different.
- **Friendship Level Up:** Kindness is like the ultimate friendship glue. Feeling important and loved? That's what you get when kindness is your go-to move.
- **Zapping the Meanies:** Being kind is like having a secret shield against the not-so-nice stuff, like bullying or teasing. When you're more about lifting others up instead of putting them down, the whole vibe changes. It's like turning a battleground into a playground.
- **Boosting Your Inner Hero:** And here's the cool part – being kind doesn't just make others feel great; it makes you feel like a rockstar too. When the kindness you throw out there comes back, your confidence soars. It's like your heart's doing a happy dance, and you feel top of the world. That's the power of kindness!

Alright, now that we've got the scoop on why kindness is such a game-changer, let's gear up and boost your kindness levels to epic proportions. Get ready to learn some super cool tips that'll turn you into a kindness pro, making every day a little brighter, both for you and everyone around you.

1. Unleash the Power of Your Smile:

Hey, did you know your smile is like a superpower? It doesn't cost a thing, but it can make someone's day awesome. Whether you're figuring out a tough puzzle, cheering up a buddy, or just strolling around, flash that grin of yours. It's like a sunshine ray on a cloudy day. So next time you're on a videocall, walking to school, or deep in a game, remember, your smile is your secret weapon to spread some serious joy.

2. Master the Magic Words: 'Thank You':

You might be thinking, "Thank you? That's no big deal." But you'd be surprised how those two little words can work like magic. It's about showing you notice the cool stuff others do for you, and you appreciate it. It's more than just good manners; it's about making someone feel valued. So, whether it's your teacher who helped you out, a friend who passed the ball to you, or someone holding the door, drop a 'thank you' and watch their face light up. It's like casting a spell of happiness – simple, yet super powerful.

3. Championing Selfless Super Moves:

You know those super cool things you do without expecting anything back, like helping someone or sharing your snacks? Those are your selfless super moves, and they're a big deal. When you do something just to make someone else's day better, it's like you're a real-life hero. So, next time you do something awesome for some-one, give yourself a pat on the back. It's these little acts of kindness that make you stand out as a genuinely cool person. Plus, the more you do it, the more it becomes your signature move!

4. Speak with Kindness, Be a Leader:

Ever notice how words can be like magic spells? They can lift someone up or bring them down. At home, make sure you're using words that are like a high-five, not a put-down. Instead of getting mad right away, try explaining things in a cool, calm way. It's like being the captain of a ship – guiding, not bossing around. This shows that kindness isn't just about what you do; it's also about what you say. And when you lead by example, you're teaching everyone around you how to be a kindness pro, too. It's about showing that everyone's feelings matter and that there's always a kind way to handle stuff, even when it's tough.

5. Mastering the Art of the Apology:

Saying "sorry" when you mess up is like hitting the reset button – it can fix things that went a bit sideways. If you accidentally hurt someone's feelings, it's super important to own up and apologize. It's not just about saying the words, but really understanding how your actions affected someone else. It's like being a detective in your own life, figuring out where things went wrong, and then doing your best to make it right. This shows you're not just brave but also super considerate and kind.

6. Disagreeing Like a Pro:

Disagreements happen, it's part of life. But did you know you can disagree with someone and still be total buds? It's all about how you handle it. Here are some cool moves to keep disagreements friendly and constructive:

- **Learn from the Pros:** Watch how grown-ups you respect handle their disagreements. It's like getting a sneak peek at how to keep things cool even when opinions clash.
- **Talk It Out, Peacefully:** If you feel yourself getting heated, take a deep breath. It's like hitting the pause button before things get too wild. Use calm words to express your side, like, "I see it differently because..."
- **Choices for Challenges:** When you're not seeing eye-to-eye with someone, remember you've got options. You can use 'I' messages to express yourself, take a break from the chat,

find a middle ground, or even ask a grown-up for some advice.

- **Think About What Matters Most:** Ask yourself, "Do I want to win this argument, or keep my friendship awesome?" Sometimes, what you're arguing about isn't as important as your friendship.
- **Disagreeing with Dignity:** Need the right words to disagree without causing a storm? Try starting with, "I get what you're saying, but here's my take..." or "I'm not sure I agree, but tell me more about your side."

Remember, it's totally possible to have different views and still be cool with each other. It's all about respect, understanding, and knowing that two people can see things differently and still both be right.

Spotlight on Mother Teresa: A Legacy of Kindness

Let's zoom in on someone who truly knew how to turn kindness into a superpower – Mother Teresa. She wasn't just a regular person; she was like a kindness superhero, touching lives and spreading warmth and care around the globe. Her story isn't just inspiring; it's a real-life example of how being kind can change the world, one act at a time.

Mother Teresa dedicated her life to helping those who were often forgotten by society – the sick, the poor, and the lonely. She showed that even the smallest acts of kindness, like a warm meal, a kind word, or a gentle touch, can light up someone's world. She believed that every person was important and deserved love and respect.

leading by example

Ever wonder why being a leader is such a cool thing? Well, it's like having a super toolbox that helps you tackle all sorts of adventures.

When you've got leadership skills, you're in the driver's seat of your own life, making things happen and turning ideas into real-life action. Let's break it down and see how stepping up as a leader can turn you into an everyday hero:

- **Confidence Booster:** Being a leader is like wearing a cape of confidence. It helps you believe in yourself and your ideas, giving you the courage to stand up, speak out, and shine bright.
- **Creative Problem Solver:** As a leader, you're like a master inventor. You look at problems and see them as puzzles to solve, coming up with creative and super cool solutions that others might not have thought of.
- **Teamwork Champion:** Leadership isn't just about going solo; it's about rallying the troops and rocking it as a team. It's about knowing how to bring out the best in everyone, making sure the whole squad is moving forward together.
- **Collaboration King:** Great leaders know that two heads (or more!) are better than one. They're awesome at working with others, sharing ideas, and making plans that are way cooler because everyone's involved.
- **Responsibility Rockstar:** And here's a big one – being a leader means you're top-notch at handling responsibility. It's like being the captain of your ship, making sure everything's running smoothly and everyone's on track.

Here's your ultimate guide to showing off your awesome skills and making a real difference. Let's dive in!

1. Chase Your Dreams and Spark Inspiration: Got a passion or a hobby that makes you jump out of bed in the morning? Go for it! Dive into what you love, and don't be shy to share your excitement. Your zest can light a spark in others too!

2. Stand Strong with Your Values: Know what you stand for and let those values shine in everything you do. Whether it's fairness, courage, or kindness, your solid values are like your personal compass, guiding you and inspiring your buddies.

3. Be a Community Hero: Remember, being a leader isn't just about you; it's about lifting everyone up. Find ways to help out, support your mates, and make your corner of the world a bit brighter. It's about being a team player in the big game of life.

4. Share the Love and Welcome Everyone: A true champ knows that there's room for everyone in the winner's circle. Be open-hearted, welcome new ideas, and celebrate what makes each person unique. It's like building a super team where everyone's a star.

5. Tackle Challenges Like a Pro: Life can throw some curveballs, but guess what? You've got what it takes to knock them out of the park. Show how you face obstacles head-on, learn from them, and come out stronger. It's about turning 'oops' into 'a-ha' moments!

And here are some everyday super moves to keep you on top of your game:

- **Cheer On Their Passions:** When your pals are into something, be their biggest fan. It's like being part of their personal cheer squad.
- **Listen Like a Boss:** Hear out their ideas and stories without any 'buts' or 'however.' It's about giving them the stage and showing you're all ears.

- **Share Your Wisdom, But Only When Asked:** Sometimes, a nudge in the right direction is all they need. Offer your two cents, but only when they're shopping for advice.
- **Be Their Teammate, Not Just Their Leader:** Remind them you're in this together, side by side. It's about sharing the journey, not just leading the way.
- **Guide Them Through Life's Big Questions:** Whether it's college, careers, or the next big step, be their Google map, helping them navigate through.
- **Model Super Social Skills:** Show off your best moves in coping, caring, and being grateful. It's about being a live demo of awesomeness in action.
- **Keep the Chat Zone Positive:** No room for downers or harsh words in your conversations. It's all about good vibes and constructive chats.
- **Encourage Open Hearts and Open Minds:** Being real and sharing feelings is where it's at. Show them it's cool to be true to yourself and your emotions.
- **Hand Out Handy Tips for Everyday Heroics:** Share your secrets for being a day-to-day superstar, showing how little things can make a big impact.

With these tips in your utility belt, nobody can stop you from being the best leader out there!

Empathy and Understanding Different Perspectives

Empathy is like having super vision that lets you see and feel what others are going through. It's what makes you hand over your favorite action figure to your little brother when he's upset or sit next to a buddy who's feeling low. When you're good at empathy, you're not just understanding others; you're showing them they matter. Here's how you can power-up your empathy skills:

Chat About Feelings: Make talking about emotions as normal as chatting about your favorite game or sport. It helps you tune into your own feelings and understand your friends' and family's emotions too.

By putting feelings into words, you're training to be an empathy ninja, ready to understand and help out, whether it's cheering up your sad teammate or being there for your family.

Boosting Empathy Through Imagination and Stories

Role-playing and diving into books are like secret missions to supercharge your empathy. They're not just fun; they're your ticket to understanding all the wild, wonderful, and wacky feelings people can have. Ready to step into someone else's shoes and see the world through their eyes? Let's roll!

- **Dive into Pretend Play:** Imagine you're an actor on a mission to explore new roles and emotions. Pretend play is your stage, where you can be anyone, from a superhero to a new kid in school. When you're in character, think about how they might feel in different situations. It's like having an empathy workout, flexing your feelings muscles and understanding others better.
- **Be the Star in Different Stories:** You can turn any regular day into a scene from a movie. What would you do if you were the new kid, the brave adventurer, or the genius inventor? It's not just about the action; it's about feeling the part too.
- **Jump into the Pages of a Book:** Books are like empathy treasure chests, each page brimming with emotions and adventures. When you read, you're not just following a story; you're walking in the characters' shoes, feeling their highs and lows.

- **Spot the Feelings:** As you read, play detective with the characters' emotions. Are they jumping with joy, shivering with fear, or scratching their heads in confusion? Talk about these feelings and think about what you'd do if you were in their place.

By role-playing and reading, you're not just having fun; you're becoming an empathy expert, learning how to connect, understand, and be there for others.

interaction - your very own kindness journal

How about starting a super cool project, like your very own Kindness Journal? It's like being a kindness detective, tracking down all the awesome things you do each day. Whether it's lending a hand, sharing a smile, or dropping a nice word, every act of kindness is a clue that leads to becoming an even greater you.

Here's how you can make your Kindness Journal the best book on your shelf:

- **Daily Kindness Mission:** Every day, set out on a mission to do something kind. Big or small, every act counts.
- **Journal Time:** At the end of the day, grab your journal and jot down what you did. It's like collecting trophies of your awesome deeds.
- **Detail Detective:** Don't just write what you did; dive into how it made you feel and how it might have brightened someone else's day.
- **Look Back and Reflect:** Every now and then, flip through your journal. You'll see how all those kind acts add up to a whole lot of awesome.

Keeping a Kindness Journal isn't just about remembering what you've done; it's about seeing how every bit of kindness you spread makes the world a cooler, happier place. Ready to start jotting down your journey of kindness? Let's turn the page and begin!

Alright, you're now all clued up on why kindness rocks, how to be a leader who leads with heart, and how to keep track of all the awesome you're spreading around. You've got the tools, the know-how, and the superpowers to make kindness your signature move. But don't just keep it in these pages – take it out into the world and watch how it transforms not just your day, but everyone's around you.

But guess what? There's more! Coming up next, we're going to take all these cool skills and show you how they're not just about being awesome today; they're about setting you up for a lifetime of success. Get ready to connect the dots!

8 /
preparing for
success

E ver catch yourself daydreaming about what you want to be
when you grow up? Maybe you see yourself scoring the
winning goal, inventing something mind-blowing, or helping
people in a big way. But ever wonder how you get from here to
there? Success isn't just about the finish line; it's about the amazing
race you run to get there. It's about setting your goals, tackling challenges like a boss, and turning your dreams into reality.

In this chapter, we're not just going to dream about success; we're
going to start building the path to make it all happen. Whether you
want to be a sports star, a science whiz, or a hero in your community, it all starts with a plan, some serious skills, and the courage to
chase after your dreams. Ready to map out your journey to success
and take the first step? Let's hit the road and turn your dreams into
your future!

defining personal success

Hey, did you wonder about what success really means to you? It's not just about what everyone else thinks or the stuff you can show off. It's way deeper. It's about setting your own goals, the kind that make you jump out of bed in the morning, excited to start the day. Success is like your personal victory dance – it's how you feel when you know you're nailing it, in your own unique way.

Whether it's being a part of a team, helping out in your community, or just getting better at something you love, success is all about reaching those goals that mean the most to you. It's like having your own secret recipe for awesomeness. So, what's your version of success? Is it hitting a home run, acing a test, or maybe making a new friend? Remember, success isn't one-size-fits-all; it's whatever makes you feel like a champ. Let's take a moment to think about what makes you feel on top of the world and how you can chase after that feeling every day!

Let's dive into some super cool exercises that can help you discover your passions and get to know yourself a bit better. Ready? Let's go!

1. **Show-and-Tell Time:** Grab your favorite things and share why they're special to you. It's a fun way to realize what you love most!
2. **Journaling Journey:** Write down your thoughts and dreams. It's like having a chat with yourself and discovering what makes you tick.
3. **Hopes and Dreams List:** Jot down all the awesome stuff you want to do or achieve. Dream big – the sky's the limit!
4. **Try Something New:** Dive into a new hobby or activity. You never know – your next big passion might be just around the corner.

5. **Practice Gratitude:** Every day, think of a few things you're thankful for. It helps you see the awesome stuff in your life.

6. **Positive Affirmations:** Speak kind, encouraging words to yourself. It's like being your own cheerleader!

7. **Read about Self-Awareness:** Dive into books that help you understand your feelings and thoughts. It's like going on an adventure inside your own mind.

8. **Make a Vision Board:** Create a collage of pictures and words that represent your dreams and goals. It's your future, on display!

9. **Role Playing:** Act out different scenarios and explore how you might feel and react. It's like trying on different hats and seeing which one fits best.

10. **Create a Self-Awareness Box:** Fill a box with items that represent you. It's like a treasure chest of 'you'!

11. **Emotional Check-Ins:** Take a moment to think about how you're feeling throughout the day. It's like being a weather reporter for your emotions.

12. **Practice Mindfulness:** Spend some quiet time just being present in the moment. It helps you tune into yourself and the world around you.

13. **Drawing to Show Emotions:** Use colors and doodles to express how you're feeling. It's like painting your emotions!

14. **Write a Short Story:** Create a tale with you as the main character. Where will your adventures take you?

15. **Letter to Future Self:** Write a letter to 'future you.' What do you want to tell or ask yourself?

16. **Learn to Pray:** If it's part of your tradition, praying can be a quiet time for reflection and connection.

17. **Reflect on Past Decisions:** Think about choices you've made – what you learned from them and how they shaped you.

18. **Question Assumptions:** Challenge what you think about yourself. Are there new sides of you waiting to be discovered?
19. **Seek Wise Counsel:** Chat with someone you trust and respect. Their insights can be like a guiding light.
20. **Reflect on Stereotypes:** Think about any labels you use or hear. Are they really true or just a cover for something more?
21. **Celebrate Your Uniqueness:** Remember, there's only one you! Celebrate what makes you special and different.

With these exercises, you're not just learning about your passions – you're on a journey to discovering the awesome, one-of-a-kind person you are. Ready to explore and shine?

Let's check out some incredible stories of people who turned their dreams into reality, showing us that success truly has many faces.

- **Steve Jobs: The Comeback King of Tech** Imagine being kicked out of your own treehouse, only to climb back and make it a castle! That's what happened to Steve Jobs with Apple. He faced some tough times, but his curiosity and passion for innovation kept him going. He made a grand comeback and took Apple to the top, showing us that sometimes, the road to success has a few detours.
- **J.K. Rowling: The Magical Mind Behind Harry Potter** Picture getting your super cool story turned down not once but loads of times. That's what happened to J.K. Rowling with her Harry Potter books. But she didn't let those "No's" stop her. She believed in her magical world of wizards and, guess what? Her persistence paid off big time, turning her story into a global sensation. It's like her own spell of success!

- **Michael Jordan: From Rejection to Legend** Ever been told you're not tall enough, fast enough, or just enough? Michael Jordan knows that feeling. He was actually cut from his high school basketball team! But did he give up? No way! He practiced like a hero, fueled by his love for the game, and soared to become one of the greatest players ever to hit the court. It's like he turned a missed shot into a slam dunk of success.

These stories aren't just about winning; they're about not giving up, chasing your dreams, and being the best you can be, no matter what.

developing problem-solving skills

Ready for a little secret? In the big adventure of life, you're going to run into some bumps on the road. Yep, it's true. But here's the cool part: those bumps aren't just obstacles; they're chances to grow, learn, and become even more awesome. So, it's super important to gear up with some top-notch problem-solving skills and learn how to keep your cool when things get a bit wobbly. Let's dive into how you can become a pro at tackling those tricky moments and turn them into your victory laps.

When you're out there facing life's puzzles, it's like being a detective on a super cool mission. Let's break down the steps to crack the case of any problem that comes your way. And remember, every detective needs their trusty notebook and a team of sidekicks. Ready? Let's solve this!

1. **Spot the Problem:** First up, put on your detective hat and figure out exactly what the mystery is. It's like finding the missing piece of your favorite puzzle.

2. **Think Tank Time:** Gather your brainiest ideas on how to solve the puzzle. Imagine you're the brainstorming boss, coming up with all sorts of wild and wonderful solutions.

3. **Test Drive a Solution:** Pick one of your brilliant ideas and give it a whirl. It's like choosing the right key to unlock a treasure chest. If it clicks, awesome! If not, no sweat.

4. **Trial and Error:** If the first key doesn't fit, don't worry. It's all part of the adventure. Head back to your list of solutions and try the next one. It's like being a scientist doing super cool experiments.

While you're on this detective journey, keep these handy tips in mind:

- **Peek Into the Past:** Sometimes, the clue you need is in an old case you've already solved. Flip back through your past adventures and see if there's a trick you've missed.

- **Keep a Blooper Reel:** Write down what didn't work. It's not just about keeping track; it's about learning what to skip next time.

- **Team Up:** When the case gets tricky, don't go solo. Ask for advice from your trusted crew – friends, family, or anyone you look up to. Sometimes, they see clues you might miss.

Cool Stories of Problem-Solving Heroes

Let's zoom into some real-life action where heroes just like you used their super problem-solving skills to save the day. Their adventures are not just about winning; they're about learning and growing smarter every step of the way.

Evelyn: The Eco-Hero CEO

Imagine being in charge of a company that helps the planet, and you've got a chance to make it even cooler by getting a hotel in a place as awesome as Costa Rica. Evelyn was in this exact spot. But here's the twist: her team had different ideas about how to move forward. So, what did she do? She tuned into her team's super skills, made sure everyone was heard, and guided them like a captain steering a ship through stormy seas. The result? Less fuss, more teamwork, and a decision that made everyone high-five.

The Lightning-Fast Problem Solver

Now, picture someone who's like a detective and a ninja rolled into one. This problem-solving whiz at Lightning Problem Solving knows that to crack a case, you've got to dig deep and find the real cause, not just the stuff on the surface. He's all about being smart, not just busy. Instead of just sitting around and having super long talks, he gets to the heart of the problem, figures it out, and then takes action. It's like having a secret shortcut to success.

These stories aren't just cool tales; they're like your personal guide on how to tackle problems head-on, understand what's really going on, and find the smartest, slickest way to solve them!

planning for the future

Setting goals is like having your very own game plan for winning at sports, acing your classes, and pretty much rocking at life? Yep, it's true! Whether you're dreaming of scoring the winning goal or building the coolest robot, having goals is like having a treasure map that leads you to success. Let's check out why setting goals is super important and how it turns you into a goal-getting champ. Ready to discover your secret superpower?

- **Time Management Mastery:** Picture this: you've got a cool project or a big game coming up. Instead of waiting till the last second and rushing like a mad scientist, setting goals helps you break it down into chill, doable parts. Studies say loads of students tend to put things off, but not you! With goals, you've got a clear plan and deadlines, so you know just what to do and when to do it. It's like having a superpower that lets you dodge procrastination and use every minute like a pro.

- **Supercharging Your Confidence:** Every time you tick off a goal, it's like scoring a personal victory. You feel like a champion, realizing, "Hey, I can totally do this!" With each goal you reach, your confidence soars a bit higher. It's not just about finishing tasks; it's about seeing yourself grow and take on even cooler, bigger challenges. As you keep smashing your goals, you're not just achieving stuff; you're building the most awesome version of you.

- **No More Feeling Lost:** Ever felt like you're in the middle of a maze, not sure which way to turn? Setting goals cuts through the confusion. It's like having a plan that says, 'Hey, this is the way! Follow me!' No more feeling frustrated or overwhelmed, because you've got your path all laid out.

- **Time to Shine:** With your goals lighting the way, you can spend more time doing the cool stuff that gets you closer to your big win. It's about ditching the distractions and pouring all your energy into making your goals happen. Every step you take is a step towards something awesome you've set out for yourself.

So, whether it's building the world's coolest Lego castle, becoming a math whiz, or scoring goals on the field, remember setting goals is your secret tool.

Feel like your motivation tank is running a bit low? Totally normal! Even superheroes have days when their superpowers feel a bit snoozy. But guess what? You've got what it takes to rev up your motivation engine and keep rolling towards your goals. Let's check out some turbo-charged tips to keep your motivation high and your spirits even higher. Ready to fuel up and zoom ahead? Let's hit the gas!

- **Break It Down: Small Goals, Big Wins:** Instead of staring at a giant mountain of a goal, slice it into mini, munchable pieces. It's like turning a big pizza into bite-sized slices – way easier to tackle, and every slice is a tasty win!
- **Enjoy the Ride:** Don't just keep your eyes on the finish line; soak up the fun along the way. It's about loving the game, not just the trophy at the end. Each step you take is part of an epic adventure.
- **Surround Yourself with Cheerleaders:** Keep your squad of positive pals close. They're like your personal cheerleading team, always ready to lift you up and keep the good vibes flowing.
- **Balance Is Key:** Life's like a giant seesaw. Too much work or too much play, and things get wobbly. Find your perfect balance – some work, some play, some chill time – and watch how everything clicks into place.
- **Remember Your Super 'Why':** When the going gets tough, remind yourself why you started. It's like having a secret power-up that boosts your energy and lights up your path.
- **Count Your Wins:** Take a moment every day to think about the cool stuff you're thankful for. It's like collecting coins in a game; each one makes you richer in happiness and motivation.

And hey, on those days when motivation seems to play hide-and-seek, remember that discipline is your trusty sidekick. It's about doing the right thing, even when you don't feel like it, because you know it's good for you.

interaction - future vision board

Ready to put your dreams and goals into a super cool collage? That's right, we're talking about creating your very own Future Vision Board. It's like a treasure map that shows all the awesome stuff you want to do, be, and experience. Let's get those creative juices flowing and start picturing your amazing future. Ready to dive in and make your Vision Board the most epic one ever? Here we go!

- **Gather Your Supplies:** Grab some poster board, magazines, markers, stickers, or anything else that sparks your creativity. It's like packing for an adventure – you want all the best tools with you.
- **Dream Big:** Think about what gets you super excited. Is it becoming a sports hero, an inventor, a world traveler, or maybe a master chef? Your board is a blank canvas for your biggest, boldest dreams.
- **Cut and Paste Your Passions:** Flip through those magazines and cut out pictures and words that match your dreams. It's like putting together a puzzle where every piece is a part of your future.
- **Arrange with Flair:** Lay out your pictures and words on the board in a way that makes you smile. It's your masterpiece, so feel free to get artsy and make it pop!
- **Add Some Sparkle:** Use markers, stickers, or anything else to jazz up your board. It's all about making it shine and showing off what makes you, well, YOU!
- **Display It Proudly:** Put your Vision Board somewhere you'll see it every day. It's like having a daily reminder of

where you're headed and all the cool stuff you're going
to do.

Creating your Future Vision Board isn't just about making something pretty to look at; it's about setting your sights on your dreams
and turning 'someday' into 'heck yes, I'm doing this!' Ready to
bring your future to life, one picture at a time? Let's make it
happen!

Alright, you've got your game plan sorted, know how to dodge
those tricky problems, and have a super cool Vision Board that's
like a snapshot of your future awesomeness. Guess what? You're all
set to turn those dreams into your everyday reality! With your
strategies, smarts, and a clear picture of where you're headed,
there's nothing standing in your way. You're like a superhero, ready
to leap over any obstacle and race towards your goals.

But hey, all this planning and dreaming isn't just for fun – it's your
blueprint for action. It's time to take all that learning, all those
ideas, and bring them to life. Whether it's acing that test, nailing
that skateboard trick, or making a new friend, you've got what it
takes to make it happen.

So, lace up your sneakers, roll up your sleeves, and get ready to
show the world what you're made of.

Every step you take, every goal you chase, is a part of your
amazing journey. Remember, the real magic happens when you
step out and turn your 'someday' into 'today.'

As we wrap up this chapter on charting your path to a successful
future, think of all the cool stuff you've learned as your personal
toolbox for life. From mastering resilience to spreading kindness,
from becoming a communication whiz to setting and smashing
your goals, you've been building a foundation that's as strong as it

is awesome. You're not just ready for life's adventures; you're set to make them epic.

But wait, there's more! As we gear up for the next chapter, we're going to bring all these pieces together. Imagine it's like the grand finale of your favorite game or the last chapter of an epic book. Let's get ready to turn the page and step into the amazing journey ahead, armed with your superpowers of resilience, kindness, communication, and goal-setting. The next chapter awaits!

a chance to help someone else

As you turn the last page of this book, I envision you taking the steps you need to build your resilience, make wonderful friendships, go for your goals, and remain 100% true to yourself. I hope you're already planning small but significant moves like signing up for that drama class, performing a few random acts of kindness, or embracing the growth mindset with zest. Even the smallest changes can have a profound effect on your life, enhancing your ability to see yourself and the world around you through a more positive lens. If so, I ask that you give someone else the chance to discover who they are and all they are capable of.

Simply by sharing your honest opinion of this book, you'll show new readers where they can harness practical strategies that they can start adopting in their lives practically from day one.

Thank you so much for your support. Go ahead and seize the day!

Scan the QR code below to leave your review on Amazon.

conclusion

Wow, what a journey we've embarked on together! It's been quite the rollercoaster, right? From standing tall and fearless in the face of bullies to honing our skills to become a whiz at solving life's puzzles, we've journeyed through the thick and thin of it. Each lesson we've tackled, every skill we've polished – they're not just neat tricks up our sleeve; they're the powerful tools that will shape our journey through life. They're like keys to doors of opportunities, waiting to be opened. So, hold these lessons close, like precious gems, because they're about to light up your path to greatness.

Think about it – we've transformed into superheroes of our own stories, equipped with the courage to face challenges head-on, the wisdom to navigate through tricky terrains, and the heart to reach out and lift others up. These skills we've mastered? They're the secret ingredients to a life well-lived, filled with adventures, successes, and the joy of overcoming the odds.

But, as we've learned, being a hero isn't just about personal triumphs; it's about extending a hand, sharing your light with those around you. Why not spread the magic? Pass on these life-changing lessons to a friend, a sibling, or even someone you've just met.

Teach them how to be unshakeable when the bullies of life try to knock them down, how to think outside the box and solve problems like a boss, and how to really listen and connect deeply in conversations.

Imagine the ripple effect when you share what you've learned. It's like lighting a candle from another; the light only grows brighter. You're not just empowering your crew; you're also reinforcing your own mastery of these skills. It's a win-win! Together, you'll create an unstoppable force, a community of problem-solvers, dream-chasers, and kind-hearted heroes ready to make the world a better place.

Hold these lessons close, wear them like armor, and step forward each day with a growth mindset. Every challenge is an opportunity to grow stronger, wiser, and more resilient. Make these skills a part of your everyday life, and watch how they transform your world, one day at a time.

I believe in you with all my heart. Whatever your dream is – whether it's scoring the winning goal, acing that test, or anything else you set your mind to – you've got what it takes to make it happen. You're not just prepared for success; you're ready to soar. So, take a deep breath, square your shoulders, and step forward. Your journey to greatness is just beginning, and I can't wait to see where it takes you!

references

EzySchooling. (n.d.). Importance of Life Skills. Retrieved from https://ezyschooling.com/parenting/expert/importance-of-life-skills

Bullying Free NZ. (n.d.). Different Types of Bullying. Retrieved from https://bullyingfree.nz/about-bullying/different-types-of-bullying/

My Online Therapy. (n.d.). Psychological Impact of Bullying. Retrieved from https://myonlinetherapy.com/psychological-impact-of-bullying/

Emerging Minds. (n.d.). In Focus: Childhood Bullying. Retrieved from https://emergingminds.com.au/resources/in-focus-childhood-bullying/

Boston Children's Hospital. (n.d.). Bullied: Samantha's Story. Retrieved from https://answers.childrenshospital.org/bullied-samanthas-story/

Big Life Journal. (n.d.). Self-Confidence Building Activities. Retrieved from https://biglifejournal.com/blogs/blog/self-confidence-building-activities

KidsHealth. (n.d.). Peer Pressure. Retrieved from https://kidshealth.org/en/kids/peer-pressure.html

VerywellFamily. (n.d.). Negative and Positive Peer Pressure: Differences. Retrieved from https://www.verywellfamily.com/negative-and-positive-peer-pressure-differences-2606643

LoveToKnow. (n.d.). Types of Peer Pressure. Retrieved from https://www.lovetoknow.com/parenting/teens/type-peer-pressure

Not Consumed. (n.d.). Consequences for Little Hearts. Retrieved from https://www.notconsumed.com/consequences-for-little-hearts/

Pear Tree School. (n.d.). Why Are Peer Relationships Important for Kids? Retrieved from https://peartree.school/why-are-peer-relationships-important-for-kids/

NSPCC. (n.d.). Sophie's Story. Retrieved from https://www.nspcc.org.uk/what-is-child-abuse/childrens-stories/sophies-story/

Big Life Journal. (n.d.). Top 35 Growth Mindset Podcasts for Families. Retrieved from https://biglifejournal.com/blogs/blog/top-35-growth-mindset-podcasts-families

Young Scot. (n.d.). 13 Ways to Support Your Friends If They Are Struggling. Retrieved from https://young.scot/get-informed/13-ways-to-support-your-friends-if-they-are-struggling/?la=north-ayrshire

Support Human. (n.d.). 8 Encouraging Things to Say to a Friend in Need. Retrieved from https://www.supporthuman.org/blog/8-encouraging-things-to-say-to-a-friend-in-need

Mind Body Green. (n.d.). How to Be a Good Friend. Retrieved from https://www.mindbodygreen.com/articles/how-to-be-a-good-friend

Firefly Therapy Austin. (n.d.). Teaching Forgiveness to Kids. Retrieved from https://www.fireflytherapyaustin.com/teaching-forgiveness-kids/

Psychology Today. (n.d.). The 13 Essential Traits of Good Friends. Retrieved from https://www.psychologytoday.com/us/blog/lifetime-connections/201503/the-13-essential-traits-good-friends#:

London Governess. (n.d.). Effective Communication Skills for Kids: Building Stronger Relationships. Retrieved from https://londongoverness.com/effective-communication-skills-for-kids-building-stronger-relationships/

Very Special Tales. (n.d.). I Statements Examples & Worksheets. Retrieved from https://veryspecialtales.com/i-statements-examples-worksheets/

Empowering Education. (n.d.). I Statements for Kids. Retrieved from https://empoweringeducation.org/blog/i-statements-for-kids/

Centers for Disease Control and Prevention. (n.d.). Active Listening. Retrieved from https://www.cdc.gov/parents/essentials/toddlersandpreschoolers/communication/activelistening.html

KidsHealth. (n.d.). Building Resilience: Help Your Child Learn to Bounce Back. Retrieved from https://kidshealth.org/en/kids/self-esteem.html

Psychology Today. (n.d.). 7 Ways to Deal with Negative Thoughts. Retrieved from https://www.psychologytoday.com/us/blog/women-s-mental-health-matters/201509/7-ways-deal-negative-thoughts

Delaware Psychological Services. (n.d.). 10 Ways to Practice Positive Self-Talk. Retrieved from https://www.delawarepsychologicalservices.com/post/10-ways-to-practice-positive-self-talk

Today. (n.d.). 50 Positive Affirmations for Kids. Retrieved from https://www.today.com/life/inspiration/affirmations-for-self-love-rcna93893

ASVAB Program. (n.d.). Building Resilience in Children. Retrieved from https://www.asvabprogram.com/media-center-article/65

Centers for Disease Control and Prevention. (n.d.). Depression in Children. Retrieved from https://www.cdc.gov/childrensmentalhealth/depression.html

Big Life Journal. (n.d.). Children and Positive Attitude: 5 Practical Tips. Retrieved from https://biglifejournal.com/blogs/blog/children-positive-attitude

Big Life Journal. (n.d.). How to Help Kids Overcome Fear of Failure. Retrieved from https://biglifejournal.com/blogs/blog/help-kids-overcome-fear-failure

Harvard Graduate School of Education. (n.d.). Learning from Mistakes. Retrieved from https://mcc.gse.harvard.edu/resources-for-families/learning-from-mistakes-2

Montessori Academy. (n.d.). Kindness Matters: Teaching Children the Importance of Kindness. Retrieved from https://montessori-academy.com/blog/kindness-matters/

Big Life Journal. (n.d.). Helping Children Build Positive Relationships. Retrieved from https://biglifejournal.com/blogs/blog/help-children-build-positive-relationships

Culture Trip. (n.d.). 10 Small Acts of Kindness That Changed the World. Retrieved from https://theculturetrip.com/europe/articles/10-small-acts-of-kindness-that-changed-the-world

Roots of Action. (n.d.). The Role of Role Models: Inspiring and Guiding Young Minds. Retrieved from https://www.rootsofaction.com/role-model/

Educator Mom Hub. (n.d.). How to Be a Good Role Model to Kids. Retrieved from https://www.educatormomhub.com/blog/how-to-be-a-good-role-model-to-kids

Big Life Journal. (n.d.). Key Strategies to Teach Children Empathy. Retrieved from https://biglifejournal.com/blogs/blog/key-strategies-teach-children-empathy

The Healthy. "Good Communication Builds Better Relationships." Accessed February 14, 2024. https://www.thehealthy.com/family/relationships/relationship-communication-quotes/

Made in United States
Troutdale, OR
11/25/2024

25217064R00092